Also by Roger Rapoport:

Is the Library Burning? (with Laurence J. Kirshbaum)

The Great American Bomb Machine

The Superdoctors

The Big Player (with Ken Uston)

*California Dreaming:
The Political Odyssey of Pat and Jerry Brown*

Into the Sunlight: Life after the Iron Curtain

Travel Books

California Catalog (with Margot Lind)

2 to 22 Days in California

2 to 22 Days in the Rockies

2 to 22 Days in Asia (with Burl Willes)

2 to 22 Days around the World (with Burl Willes)

Great Cities of Eastern Europe

Books for Children

The Wolf

The Rattler

After the Death of a Salesman

Business Trips to Hell

Roger Rapoport

RDR Books
Oakland, California

After the Death of a Salesman:
Business Trips to Hell

RDR Books
4456 Piedmont Avenue
Oakland, California 94611

ISBN 1-57143-062-8
Library of Congress Catalog Card Number: 98-065853

Cover Design: Jennifer Braham
Book Design: Paula Morrison
Editor: Bob Drews
Researchers: Erin Perry, Dawn Gray

Distributed in Canada by Orca Books 1030 North Park Street,
Victoria BC V8T 1C6

Distributed in England and Europe by Airlift Book Company,
8 The Arena, Mollison Avenue, Enfield, Middlesex EN3 7NJ
England

Distributed in Australia and New Zealand by Astam Books pty
Ltd 57–61 John Street Leichardt, New South Wales 2038, Australia

Printed in the United States of America by Thomson-Shore

To My Father

Table of Contents

Introduction . . . 1

Chapter 1. What Did Willie Loman Sell? . . . 5

Chapter 2. Foreign Travel: Innocents Abroad . . . 23

Chapter 3. Air Travel: Up Up and Oy Vey . . . 41

Chapter 4. Trade Shows: Strictly Unconventional . . . 61

Chapter 5. Women on the Road: Against All Oddballs . . . 81

Chapter 6. Lodging: Rooms with an Attitude . . . 93

Chapter 7. Short Subjects . . . 105

Chapter 8. The Back Office: Is Anybody There? . . . 117

Chapter 9. On the Town: Don't Drink to This . . . 133

Chapter 10. Sales Representatives: Life after Death . . . 141

Chapter 11. The Book Business: A Shelf Game . . . 161

Chapter 12. Short Subjects II . . . 171

Chapter 13. The Globetrotter:
Number One to Madagascar . . . 183

Chapter 14. The Final Chapter: Stolen Moments . . . 195

Author's Note . . . 199

Introduction

On the Road, Again

ON THE MORNING OF MARCH 31, 1997, a cold front swept into New England. After basking in balmy spring weather just a day earlier, the region now was under a thick blanket of snow. Drivers who had been applying sunblock to check rays pouring through their sunroofs a day earlier slalomed down icy roads. In the Berkshires, traffic on the Massachusetts Turnpike halted as tow trucks struggled to upright jackknifed big rigs. A wreck at the entrance to the Blandford rest stop forced drivers to crawl into the parking lot via the exit lane. With winds gusting to 60 miles an hour and visibility down to about 100 feet, it was obvious that the service plaza's Burger King was going to be my home for the evening. More than 100 fellow travelers, many of them locals who knew better than to challenge the icy grades, had begun staking out floor space. The Burger King crew was already planning for an all-night stand.

Just as there are no atheists in foxholes, there are few vegetarians in a blizzard at Burger King. Fat, grease, cholesterol, sugar—they all sounded like haute cuisine by 6 P.M. And that night, as I bedded down on four carefully arranged chairs, it occurred to me that this is what one of the theatergoers on the opening night of Arthur Miller's play *Death of a Salesman* meant when he said, "That New England territory never was any damn good."

What was I doing at this snowed-in Burger King? I am a salesman.

Once upon a time, this was a nation of salesmen hawking brushes, pots and pans, vacuum cleaners, encyclopedias, you name it. At one point in the late 19th century, more than 350,000 salesmen had lit out for what Huck Finn called "the territories." And in a way they brought with them the same restlessness that characterized Twain's hero. Freedom was just another word for leaving home, and that's what traveling salesmen did. They walked out on hearth and family muttering something about "responsibilities." But even when they weren't standing on the back of wagons peddling their wares, even when they showed up in three-piece suits bearing leather sample cases, they were looked on as aliens or gypsies. Outside the American experience, they represented a kind of freedom that others could only dream about. As strangers they could walk into a new town free of their past, able to operate independently and leave on a moment's notice with, hopefully, money or orders in hand. Their rootlessness fascinated literary artists who saw their story as the paradigm for the American tragedy. Sprinkle in a few coarse jokes about their magnificent obsession with farmers' daughters and you have the picture.

Today their ranks have been slashed by a variety of technologies loosely grouped under the rubric of "scientific salesmanship." Catalogs, telemarketing, discount stores and a host of other trends have largely made sidewalk warriors and door-to-door salesmen the stuff of history books. But selling through the handshake, the personal appeal, still has a place. Going beyond shoe leather, the world of the salesman and saleswoman has expanded to phones, trains, airplanes, hotels, motels and, yes, Burger Kings. The need for the human touch hasn't gone away, it has just taken on a different means of hitting the road. Where once a sales rep covered cities or counties, she now covers states, regions and even continents. This mushrooming territoriality, coupled with the universe of mass marketing, the Internet and everlasting attention to costs have created challenges, demands and opportunities for disaster that the Fuller Brush salesman could never have imagined.

My grandfather Max Goodman was a salesman—he was good but had his ups and downs that were typical of the life of the salesman in the first half of this century. "If they made a movie of his life," my Uncle Ken told me, "it would be called *After the Death of a Salesman*." The world of the 1990s has a slightly different tone—*The Deaths of a Salesman* if you will.

I am in the book business. As an independent book publisher and owner of RDR Books in Oakland, California, I travel about 100 days a year to all sections of the United States, as well as overseas to Europe. These travels haven't necessarily made me any smarter, but they have made me more knowledgeable—both about the horrors and comedies that await the salesman or saleswoman and about opportunities and challenges in the book industry today. I hope you'll indulge me on both those counts in the course of this book which follows on the heels of two related titles: *I Should Have Stayed Home: Worst Trips of Great Writers* and *I've Been Gone Far Too Long: Field Trip Fiascoes and Expedition Disasters*.

As you and I become travel companions in the pages and chapters ahead, I'll share my travel experiences and thoughts on the book business and the disaster stories of my compatriots on the road. Our intention is to be humorous and entertaining. We're not talking nuclear disarmament here. Get ready to laugh and let's go.

1

What Did Willie Loman Sell?

I USED TO WRITE BOOKS for a living. In 1993 I had a chance to publish one, then another, and now my sample case has 21 titles—women's books, kids books, humor books, travel literature—even a book of poetry. My mother had definitely not raised me to be a salesman. Our families, the Rapoports and the Goodmans, were the kind of people who didn't like to miss a paycheck. In fact you'd have to skip a generation and reach back to my Grandfather Max to find someone in either family who hit the road.

My grandfather knew how to close a deal, and that's where his successes and failures began. As I discovered on hundreds of one-night stands from Cape Cod to the Olympic Peninsula, doing business out of a sample case is the ultimate form of on-the-job training. Finding buyers, getting paid in 30 days, not breaking any laws, locating a convenient restroom before the next call—these are the heart and soul of bookselling. And as I travel and compare notes with others in the sales trade, it is obvious that people traveling overnight for work are asking the same question I shouted while pulling out of that Burger King the morning after the big storm: "When can I go home?"

For what it's worth, I am of the opinion that most business

trips begin as mistakes and end as disasters. As I boarded an Amtrak train in Holland, Michigan, (it was running so late that the conductor decided he wasn't even going to charge us for the trip to Chicago) a tagline on the front of *USA Today* announced that business travelers are cutting back on their journeys because of all the hassles of road work.

That was news to me. The fact that so many of us who should know better keep making the same mistake is proof positive of that adage, those who refuse to learn from the past are likely to flunk history.

How else to explain why I make so many business trips other than that, like so many others on the road, we haven't really found our purpose in life or learned the meaning of the word no. We keep thinking that if we turn just one more corner, we will find whatever it is that is missing in our lives. I know that's true in my case because the more time I spend in bookstores, the closer I get to the person I want to be. Strange, isn't it, how some of us can't stand still? We have to be catching a plane, renting a car and sleeping in unfamiliar beds. I remember waking up one morning in New York next to a woman I had met only the night before and asking myself if it was love or just a date that had gone out of control. Before I could begin to answer the question I was in a cab headed for the National Stationery Show. Who has time to consider such trivial matters when there is important work to be done?

In a way it was the perfect metaphor for business travel. A night here, a night there, but never too long anywhere.

Just about anyone who has ever taken a phone pitch from an MCI or AT&T salesman (Did you know that some solicitors are actually prisoners calling from inside a jail?), thrown out unwanted direct mail from Sears siding or had to say no to a credit card phone solicitor understands the problem. Salesmen are pests, they are pushy, and often are the butt of countless jokes. In art and in literature, in drama and commercials, salesmen are goofballs and buffoons, they are loud and dress funny.

Think of Woody Allen dodging an insurance salesman or a car salesman who won't let you out the door until you at least take a test drive. Even though many of them work without benefits, health insurance, a retirement plan, paid vacations or holidays given to entry-level employees, salesmen are frequently derided by their employers behind their backs and, in some instances, to their faces. Even the executives who benefit directly from their efforts diminish the quality and significance of their work. "I could have done that" is an oft-heard line when a salesman brings in a big order. This lack of respect is endemic in many businesses. When I started publishing books, one of my friends told me flat out that salesmen were "a dying breed, I'm not sure they'll be around in another 10 years. Who needs them?" Indeed my own respect for their many accomplishments is grounded largely in a career accident. I was forced to learn how to sell to start a business.

As any survey of American literature will show you, the traveling salesman—and believe me the protagonist is always a man in these short stories, novels, plays and musicals—is but one step away from the emergency room, if he's lucky. In Eudora Welty's story, *The Death of a Traveling Salesman,* Mr. Bowman is ill, exhausted and lost. He perishes among strangers in the pre-911 era when there were no helicopters to evacuate him to the nearest regional medical center. Welty and later Arthur Miller were but two of the major 20th century literary figures who turned on the light for the mobile salesperson, illuminating their existential displacement. Sherwood Anderson, Sinclair Lewis and Eugene O'Neill all chose the traveler as a weird metaphor for everything that had gone wrong with the American experiment, a kind of carnival barker with a decent wardrobe. Operating at considerable distance from the adult American trinity—work, family and commuting—these slick operators seduced and abandoned with reckless disregard for the truth. America, lock up your daughters and sons, you just never know what baubles may be inside those sample cases designed to, oh well, never mind.

From fun musicals like *Oklahoma* and *The Music Man* to plays perfect for dissection by English literature and drama majors, the traveler has become both a launching pad for careers like Welty's and a capstone for the likes of Miller. Each in their own way easily broke through what Theodore Dreiser once called the curse of fiction American style—the happy ending.

In his wise and wonderful book *100 Years on the Road: The Traveling Salesman in American Culture,* Timothy Spears suggests that the very success these road warriors had in bringing all manner of consumerism to Main Street was instrumental in their downfall. Across America, business leaders invented many ways to replace the traveler's personal selling style with perhaps the greatest oxymoron of our time: "scientific salesmanship." The thought, the very idea that something as subtle and personal as closing a deal could be depersonalized, objectified and mass marketed was the final insult to the industrious salesman who, far from hearth and home, used his considerable powers of persuasion to convince people to buy things they didn't need at prices they couldn't afford.

Efforts to cut out the middleman, the traveler, were a conceit that basically said a young person with an MBA could easily outdistance a sales professional who had invested decades logging hundreds of thousands of miles to cultivate thousands of customers. The emerging technologies of telemarketing, catalog merchandising, direct mail and, of course, advertising, were designed to do the salesman's job by simply skipping the retailer and going straight to the consumer. Their aim was to push the Main Street retailer into second class status. There would be no need to send a woman out to present the Barbie line to the local buyer because the power of advertising would force him or her to stock it. Same thing with Beanie Babies. Or to look at it another way, once you have Wal-Mart, the hearts and minds of thousands of mom and pop buyers will follow readily.

All of this was keenly presaged in American literature, on the stage, and on the screen. In the eyes of the literary artist, the traveler became the dethroned leader of the sales pack. Literally and figuratively, as Spears points out, the traveling man was "cut off from humanity."

By the 1920s authors such as Sinclair Lewis were already mining a vast audience for this point of view. Just a week after being kicked out of divinity school, his antihero Elmer Gantry found employment as a traveling salesman. You know the rest of the story. Spears suggests that there are solid literary reasons for casting Gantry as a salesman rather than a bus driver or a short-order cook. After all, it is the salesperson who is the booster rocket for any new enterprise. Without him there is no work for the rest of us. Few can play his role, which often amounts to making something out of nothing, stealing market share from a competing product or being a service provider that gets the job done just fine. The fact that there is often no real need for the product he is promoting makes no difference. And whenever supply outstrips demand, which is frequently the case, there's bound to be trouble.

It is convenient to blame the sales or marketing people for

any business problem. There is a natural antipathy between the public at large and the purveyors of goods. The creator of the goods can't understand why they aren't selling faster. The buyer always wants a better deal. Friction is common and anger seems perfectly understandable. Careers and jobs are on the line. And keep in mind that a consumer society can only work if everyone is persuaded to want more than they have.

As Spears explains, the salesman has become, in the eyes of many artists, the point man for an entire body of literature indicting consumer society. Gantry is important because his career embraces the very forces of "scientific salesmanship" that undermined the primacy of travelers. "As drawn by Lewis," he points out, "Gantry was not only a drummer; he was a salesman, preacher, hedonist, con man, and advertiser all at once.... The traveling man's apparent death as an individual underscored his alienation from community and family life; seen as victim and exile, he presented a powerful, if mute, commentary on the demands of the market."

Spears believes this kind of fiction and the works of Welty and Thornton Wilder in *Heaven's My Destiny* exist as a kind of literary "rejoinder to a profession that exacted mind, body and soul from its practitioners." In Welty's case the death of the salesman "performs a dual function; it highlights the life-sapping demands of the profession and, by returning the sales-man to humanity, effaces his singular commercial identity."

Not so with O'Neill. In *The Iceman Cometh*, salesman Hickey murders his wife because he can't handle her willingness to forgive him for the sins he has committed on the sales road. At the play's end he is led away by the cops to death row.

Is there any chance that the endless appeal of plays like this one and Miller's, the success of novels such as *Elmer Gantry* and Dreiser's *Sister Carrie* have as much to say about their audiences as they do about their creators? Literary careers have jumpstarted on the strength of a negative portrayal of a salesman. The fact that none of these authors appears to have much experience at selling on the road themselves makes all this intriguing. Consider Penguin's unexpurgated edition of Dreiser's *Sister Carrie.* Just about everyone in the Indiana author's life, from his boss at the *Toledo Blade* who suggested that he try his hand at fiction, to his wife and his Doubleday editors, cut down the original manuscript. But in the carefully restored original, the story is darker and Drouet the seductive drummer who lures Carrie from the sticks to the corrupt metropolis becomes a bigger and less likable jerk.

Dreiser's bitter novel, loosely based on the story of his sister Emma, who had run away to New York with a married man, makes the traveling salesman about as appealing as Jack the Ripper.

It is the salesman who motivates Carrie to employ the ruse of sisterhood in the name of pure lust. It is the salesman who lures into his love nest with fine garments and wonderful meals. It is the salesman who introduces his pretend "sister" to a creep who carries her off to New York and Montreal with stolen money. "This crime," writes critic Alfred Kazin, "masterfully illustrates Dreiser's deep belief that we do what a 'voice' in us tells us to do" and of course that voice is the felon within us that "everything in our conscious minds and our civilization tries to suppress. The true source and inspiration of our actions is always illegitimate. Civilization is an ordeal. Inwardly, we are always in flight."

In the eyes of so many giants of American literature, salespeople are on the run from what they are doing to the rest of us. It is almost as if they are escaping from the crimes they are committing on the road, running from their customers, just one step ahead of the posse. Strangely though, I didn't see any red police gumballs flashing behind me as I traveled across the Southern California desert, loving my job, enjoying my customers, proud of the books people were putting on their shelves, feeling good about the authors who created these stories and the readers who would buy them. At the end of the day, sitting back at one of my all time favorite restaurants, George's at the Cove in La Jolla, I felt happy and fulfilled, happier actually than in my previous careers as author, travel writer and journalist. I enjoyed publishing the books **and** selling them myself.

In the town of Hemet, I had presented our titles at a bookshelf in the middle of Cameron's, a jammed bookstore where the cash register never stopped ringing during my hour-long visit. I even bought a two cassette play, by Arthur Miller, certainly one of the most famous 20th-century alumni of my alma mater, the University of Michigan.

Driving back across the desert, the horizon went sky blue pink as I made my way southeast through "the territories" to San Diego. The story emerging from the Dodge tapedeck had a familiar ring. Willie Loman, already reduced from salary to straight commission and no benefits, was in the process of being fired by his Yuppie boss. Talk about a wrongful termination case. Thirty-four years with the company. Breach of oral contract. Intentional infliction of emotional distress. In today's business world, the matter would never even reach trial. There would be an easy six figure out of court settlement, more than enough to pay for a retirement loaded with fun remodeling projects, hydroponic gardening and plenty of time to dote on those cute little chips off the block courtesy of Biff and Hap's wonderful wives. Thanks to guaranteed COBRA health benefits and Medicare, Linda and Willie wouldn't even need to worry about Prozac bills or the price of family therapy. Talk about a happy ending. Hollywood would just love it.

By the time I reached my hotel in La Jolla, I was running late, as usual, for a phone appointment. My Uncle Cal, after some weeks of discussion, had agreed to move into terra incognita—the story of my grandfather Max Goodman. Everyone in my family talked about my grandfather in a guarded way, little pieces of the truth leaked out here and there in the manner of a chemical factory that had just been designated a Superfund cleanup site by the Environmental Protection Agency. But even now, 20 years after his death, specifics were hard to come by. As my Uncle Cal narrated the story, it wasn't hard to see why.

In a clear case of life imitating art, my grandfather's career fits neatly inside the popular art of apocalyptic salesmanship. In many ways it was the perfect job for a man who moved with his family to Chicago from his native Smargon, a Russian village on the road between Vilnius and Kiev, when he was just 3 years old. Like the rest of his family, he had come thanks to the intervention of his two older sisters Katie and Anna. Living in a village where Jewish children were not allowed to attend school, sister Katie joined a rebel band. Stuffing pillows beneath their bed sheets to fool their father when he checked the children each night, Katie climbed out windows to attend subversive meetings. Eventually she fled to the United States to escape a jail sentence for revolutionary activity.

In her early 20s, Katie arrived in the United States and went to work in a sweatshop, saving money to send for her family. First to arrive was her sister Anna, who joined her in the garment industry. She and Katie put together enough money to bring the rest of their family to Chicago, including Max, his two other sisters and their parents. A school dropout in third grade, my grandfather always insisted that he needed to help the family matriarchy. Raised on the city's west side, Max went to work as a cab driver, occasionally lying about his age to make himself appear older. This fiction extended to the day of his wedding because he didn't want anyone to know that he was three years younger than my grandmother, Rose.

Growing up in a family of Russian Jewish emigres who dubbed themselves anarchists, Max became familiar with phrases like "freedom to the individual" and "end tyranny of the czars." They denounced strong centralized government, spoke grandly of "grass-roots societal and economic plans" and supported the Russian revolution.

He was not a radical like his sister Anna, who, after leaving a failed marriage, traveled to Russia to be part of the 1905 Revolution. Anna's travels eventually led her to Vladivostok where she was stranded in the chaos. One of my grandmother's cousins, assigned to Russia with the U.S. Marines, found her by chance at the post office in Vladivostok. Rescued and taken home on an American ship, she was repatriated to Chicago. During her long journey, Anna had fallen in love with a Russian man. Some years later, depressed over her inability to continue this relationship, disillusioned and friendless, she committed suicide, a tragedy Max could never comprehend. It added to his own political conservatism. Because he never spoke of this tragedy, none of us in the younger generation knew any of the details until after his death.

While his sisters flirted with revolution, Max decided to try his hand at capitalism. He began his sales career in the insurance business. Like many beginners in this field, he found his new career problematic. Unless you already have an established clientele, or are willing to work four or five years for a pittance, it can be difficult to gain a footing in this field. Casting about for something immediately lucrative, he discovered the home improvement business. Self-educated and self-reliant, this field was a perfect marriage of bravado, intellect and personality. He was funny and quick with numbers, easily estimating the cost of a kitchen remodel or a roofing job. Although he was never a licensed contractor, he could have easily become one.

Because sales was his forte, he avoided the burden of management, hiring in as a sales person working for or with a responsible managing employee who was a licensed contractor. His results were excellent and so were his commissions. When business was good, as it often was, my grandmother was showered with mink stoles, cut glass and jewelry. Max and Rose took my mother and her young brothers, Cal and Ken, on extended summer vacations in the Fox Lake region of northern Illinois. He drove a nice car and smoked good cigars continuously. The product mattered less than Max's ability to sell it. In fact, like Willie Loman, a lot of people weren't even sure what my grandfather was selling. He was a master of small talk from baseball scores to the restaurant scene. He was careful to qualify each customer, making sure they could afford the job before he drove over to make a sales call. And he made sure that he only sold the customers what they really needed and wanted.

As long as Max sold he was fine. Even in the worst of the Depression he and my grandmother made a fine living selling Club Aluminum cookware. In an early version of the Tupperware Party, they would cook a gourmet dinner party for prospects. Afterwards he would show his guests how easy it was to clean the soot from a deliberately burned aluminum pot.

Max was a superb closer, a fact that easily tempted him to earn more than he deserved from each deal. Determined to get ahead, he came up with an ingenious deal few customers

could resist. His specialty was "creative" financing on feder-
ally guaranteed remodeling loans. Customers were impressed
by my grandfather's ability to raise more than the value of the
job. Here is how he did it:

First he would visit a prospect and offer to roof their home
or add siding with a low-cost FHA guaranteed loan. Then,
using the government-backed remodeling loan as cover, he
would throw in a debt consolidation package to pay off some
of the customer's outstanding bills. When the loan came through
he would use some of it for the remodel and give much of the
balance to the customer. This technique was his way of closing the deal and getting a good price for the construction work.
The customer agreed to do the job for more than it was worth
because he wanted the loan consolidation. More than one
buyer remarked, after my grandfather drove off, that the deal
sounded too good to be true.

It was. The FHA backed low-interest loans were granted
for construction, not debt consolidation. When the authorities discovered my grandfather's scam, they descended on his
home or office, only to discover he had skipped town. My
grandfather would lay low for a few months, show up in a new
town, and get back to work, after pocketing nice commissions
before it was time, once again, to disappear.

Family life hit rock bottom in the mid-'30s, shortly after
my mother enrolled at the University of Illinois. When Max
suddenly went into hiding, Rose could no longer make the
rent. My grandmother moved to Champaign with her two
young sons where the entire family shared a house and took
in a few borders. After graduation, in 1938, my parents were
married in Chicago. Unfortunately, my grandfather, on the
lam in the east, was unable to attend their wedding.

The story gets worse. My grandfather was convinced that

the solution to his problems was to form a partnership with an experienced manager. He moved to Detroit, where my father, a ceramic engineer, had just taken a job with the Detroit Jewell Stove Company. Here, at last, everything seemed to be working out fine. My grandmother, carefully saving money from a wartime job at a carburetor factory, raised the down payment for a house. Max formed a wonderful cedar shake shingle joint venture with a well connected businessman. Everything was perfect as long as he sold and his partner ran the business. When he tried to assume a managerial role, business began to founder.

The stress and strain of dealing with banks and bookkeeping, collecting overdue bills, paying taxes and endless administrative deals proved overwhelming. One on one he was a master with customers. Sadly, the big picture eluded him. Max was never able to apply his gift of gab to the delicate art of massaging a creditor's ego or supervising employees. My grandfather was the quintessential outside salesman, a roadie on America's remodeling superhighway. Taking him off sales work was like trying to run an AC appliance on DC.

My grandfather also had another problem in Michigan — a disastrous affair with his partner's wife. When my grandmother discovered his infidelity she decided to move the family to California. It was here that he was finally arrested for FHA loan fraud, tried, convicted and sent to a minimum security prison in the east. He emerged a year later with two conclusions: "Take it easy and drink a lot of water; don't sweat the small stuff."

Attempts to start new businesses sputtered and failed with my grandfather leaving his colleagues to settle large debts. Typically he would get involved in a Ponzi scheme, paying for job A with proceeds from job B. Unfortunately job B sometimes fell through, leaving his suppliers empty handed and forcing the bank to repossess his home.

As his problems grew and his income fell, my grandfather made the first of several attempts to take his own life. Carefully planned and executed, these suicide attempts were a cry for help, an effort to call attention to his seemingly insoluble business problems.

"Fortunately he wasn't really trying to kill himself," my Uncle Cal explained by phone as I looked out the motel window at the La Jolla coast. It was a cloudless night, lovers were out strolling the beach cooled by a welcome wind at the end of a scorching day. "He wanted people to like him and respect him. You could call these suicide attempts a dramatic attempt to forestall his death. It was his way of calling for sympathy and help at a very dark time. We were all lucky that he didn't slip up, that he botched these attempts."

By the time I was old enough to know what my grandfather did for a living, his death threats against himself had ended. He had settled into a more stable middle-class existence, content selling in the Los Angeles basin for reasonable commissions. The fact that his employers enjoyed a good living off his adroit salesmanship did not appear to be a cause for dismay. His willingness to lower his expectations meant he was no longer felt compelled to work beyond his abilities and live beyond his means. At one point he even hired my father, temporarily between jobs in Los Angeles.

It would be facile to reduce the sum total of his working life to a few generalizations. But I'm going to try anyway, convinced that some of his successes and failures shed a little bit of light on the reality of business life on the road. To me travel of any sort is an intoxicant. You can take people who are perfectly tranquil at home or in an office, put them in a car or on a plane and they are transformed. I know this is true because it happens to me every time I turn on the timer light, stop the newspapers and double deadbolt the front door. Even if it's only a short distance from home, I get excited. Meeting new people, seeing new places, enjoying a chance to present something interesting and different to a potential customer can be exhilarating. Each day is new and different and the serendipity of business travel is a constant source of excitement.

I know that my grandfather shared that sense of discovery, as do many business people who prefer being out of the office to sitting at their desk taking phone calls or writing memos. Unfortunately the hazards of life on the road are significant. Often you are treated so well that your self-esteem rises above the danger level.

I believe that most mistakes made in business, mine and everyone else's, are triggered by out-of-control behavior. Much of this is perpetrated by people who haven't studied Newton's third law—every action has an equal and opposite reaction. Every time you make a major change in business you must be prepared to accept the adverse consequences. Unless, or until, you can learn new skills, make new friends, develop different products and selling strategies and then patiently wait for good results, you're in a lot of trouble. As a business journalist who has written for the *Wall Street Journal,* the *San Jose Mercury News,* the *Oakland Tribune* and many magazines, I can tell you that the idea, the very notion of overnight success in America is securely rooted on the fiction side of the Dewey Decimal System.

For every "instant" millionaire there are countless stories like my grandfather's. In his case moving from sales to management would have taken years. He needed to learn something about accounting, management and banking, take a few business courses, read some books, hire a consultant or two and then be prepared to wait years for good results. With very few exceptions, there is no such thing as instant gratification in the business world.

Why wouldn't my grandfather settle for less? Why did he feel the necessity of beating the system and making the kind of big money reserved for only a fortunate handful of owners and key managers? The answer is easy—coming in off the road each day he was convinced that a hot salesman could easily become a big *macher*, Yiddish for kingpin. And here is the rub. The skills needed to sell a product are not necessarily the same ones required to manage a business. My grandfather spent most of his life proving this, and only in retirement, when he became the successful leader of a senior center in the San Fernando Valley north of Los Angeles, did he begin to score on the managerial side.

His volunteer position was a perfect use of his bluster and bravado, wheeling and dealing for senior services with cunning, intellect and humor. With income out of the picture, he was at the peak of his powers. Mayor Sam Yorty's office frequently called on him to produce bus loads of enthusiastic seniors to testify for legislation that would benefit them and other older residents at the municipal level.

One of his proudest moments came in Sacramento when he testified before the California Public Utilities Commission on behalf of a reduced "lifeline" phone rate for seniors. A consummate advocate and salesman, his comments were well received by the commissioners. The lifeline plan was approved and made it possible for hundreds of thousands of seniors and low-income Californians to enjoy vital phone service that could have been beyond their reach. His work on this cause and others like it netted a wall full of plaques that he proudly displayed in his San Fernando Valley apartment. At my grandparents' 60th wedding anniversary, Yorty's office even sent a representative to hand over another plaque to Max and Rose. It was a small thank you for a job well done for the community's seniors.

"And I want to congratulate Max and Sam, for their ..." began the mayor's man as one of my cousins shouted from the back row:

"Rose, it's Rose."

Without missing a beat the deputy cranked up for a second pass: "And I want to congratulate Sam and Rose ..."

I thought of that moment, a story often retold at family reunions, as my Uncle Cal the business consultant spoke about my grandfather's career. "There is a tendency in every business to try to grow faster than you can afford." As my grandfather discovered again and again, the opportunity to grow nearly always exceeds the amount of capital necessary to realize your ambitions. He tried just a little too hard.

While Jews don't believe in the great beyond, I can imagine my grandfather, at least in spirit, chortling as you read this. He's probably even working on a new and even better deal. But that's not why we are here. Whatever you may think of him, Max's life — and those of his literary and real-life cousins — strikes at the essence of the traveling salesman: the trip that goes awry, the connection missed, the grand plan doomed, the story waiting to be told. Truly, every business trip is an accident waiting to happen, and a traveler's tale in the making.

2

Innocents Abroad

In spring 1967, Port Harcourt, the capital of rebel southeastern Nigerian states that had declared themselves the independent nation of Biafra, was not a good place for a 34-year-old American oilman like Jack Howard. Civil war between the Biafran Ibo tribe in the south and the Nigerian Hausa in the north had turned the landscape into one of the most deadly places on the planet. The fighting centered on three issues: 1) a longstanding tribal hatred, 2) The Ibos were Christian and the Hausas were Moslem, 3) The Ibos had recently discovered oil and didn't want to share it with the rest of Nigeria.

Like other dependents, Howard's wife Pat and his children had already been evacuated. Because of the fighting, he had no idea where they were or how they were coping. "I knew they were worried about my safety," says Howard, "but I had no way of contacting them."

Because all the male Biafran Ibo of fighting age were at the front, teenage girls were guarding Port Harcourt. Each day Howard had to pass seven roadblocks on his five mile drive to the office. "Young girls with loaded rifles would order us out of our cars at every roadblock," he recalls. "While two or three trained their rifles on us, the others would search us and our cars. It wouldn't have been so bad if the girls had known how to handle guns, but most obviously they had no training and there was a constant danger that we would be shot by accident."

Someone had told the girls that shoes were excellent hiding places. This meant that Howard and his Western colleagues had to take off their shoes during the search, not a lot of fun during the rainy season when ankle deep mud covered the roadway. "Body searches were always one of the high points of the day," he recalls, "especially if they were conducted during a driving rainstorm."

To up the ante, both Biafra and Nigeria had hired mercenary soldiers and pilots. In the previous African war in the Belgian Congo, many of these mercenaries had fought for the same cause. Now they were evenly divided on opposing sides. "Out of professional courtesy," Howard explains, "they tried not to shoot at each other any more than necessary."

Howard became acquainted with several of the mercenary pilots, often stopping by a local hotel after work to have a drink with them. Earning about $3,000 per month paid directly to a Swiss account, most of these 40 something fighters were German or Czech veterans of World War II. Howard had the impression that in peacetime these mercenaries would have made their living as criminals.

Each of the pilots had one thing in common, a $50,000 insurance policy furnished by their African employers. This turned out to be very good planning for the men who flew commandeered Nigerian Airways Fokker Friendship passenger planes and a matched pair of B-25's. Biafra's lone jet stayed on the ground. It was kept at the ready to evacuate the Biafran leader, Lt. Col. Ojukwo, to Europe if he decided not to fight to the death.

The pilots made life in the offshore oil fields tricky for Howard and his colleagues. One of the worst, a B-25 pilot nicknamed

Kamikaze Brown, attacked a supply workboat as it chugged out to a floating oil rig. Fortunately he missed, which was often the case because these weren't exactly modern warplanes.

"The usual bombing strategy required the pilot to fly low over the troops on the ground," remembers Howard, "while two Biafran soldiers in the back pitched hand grenades out the open passenger door. The first week this method was tried, a Fokker blew up in midair. Everyone assumed that one of the bombardiers had missed the doorway with his grenade."

Instead of rethinking their strategy, the Biafran Air Force compounded its problems with one of the most dubious bombing runs in military history. The Nigerian capital of Lagos had been off-limits for good reason. This was the only city in the land with effective anti-aircraft guns. But one night, several pilots enjoying a wild party decided it would be fun to wind up their evening with a bombing run on Lagos. Four pilots and several of their Ibo girlfriends piled into a Fokker Friendship and set a course for the capital. The women were thrilled at the idea of becoming honorary bombardiers. The Biafrans blew up a pair of oil storage tanks before being shot down. In the wreckage, the investigators found all four pilots and numerous girls. Biafrans woke up the next morning to learn their nation had just lost half its pilots, definitely a turning point in the war.

By late July, Howard and the rest of the expatriate community had come up with three evacuation plans to escape Port Harcourt. Working with a carefully concealed shortwave radio, they began working out their strategy with brief transmissions to the American Embassy in Lagos. In early August, Howard and his colleagues received a brief embassy message to evacuate because a Nigerian fleet was leaving Lagos for what would be the final invasion of Port Harcourt.

"My route out was by helicopter to an abandoned offshore oil rig. The plan was to get as many men as possible out to the rig and then arrange for a boat to come from Lagos to rescue us. Other men were to be loaded onto a dockside workboat that would slip out under cover of darkness. The remaining men, who for various reasons couldn't get out by helicopter or boat, would escape by car and then try to cross the front lines by foot.

"I was on the first helicopter load that went out to the rig. There were four of us plus the pilot on board. We had just taken off when our French pilot got a brief transmission from his base that a mercenary flying a B-25 was on his way to shoot us down as an enemy plane." Although this wasn't true, Howard and his fellow passengers kept a careful eye out for the B-25 as they headed out through the Niger Delta bayous slightly above treetop level. At the rig the chopper pilot said he was not returning to the mainland and threw in his lot with the Americans.

Back in Port Harcourt, the 50 men waiting for their helicopter evacuation received the bad news. They quickly put together a 15-car convoy and headed for Onitsha, 125 miles north of Port Harcourt and site of the sole bridge across the Niger River dividing federal and Biafran forces. Unfortunately the bridge was mined by both sides and unusable.

One of the 50 men in the convoy was a local Bank of America branch manager. On his way out of Port Harcourt, he had thoughtfully stopped off at work and helped himself to all the money in the vault. At each Army checkpoint, the manager handed the guards armfuls of money to let the convoy through. Luckily the money lasted until Onitsha where the men hired villagers to take them across the Niger in dugout canoes.

Meanwhile, the men escaping via workboat were dropped

off in the back country. They waited until dark and then began trekking through back bayous and mangrove swamps to the open ocean. Two days later the vessel arrived safely in Lagos and the expatriate oil workers caught flights home. Out on the oil rig, Howard, his three colleagues and the pilot were running out of food. Miraculously a local fisherman pulled up to the rig and agreed to take the men to shore two miles away, where a local guide led the group through the jungle to a village where they spent the night. The following morning the men hiked to a grass airstrip. "There was a lone dispatcher on duty," says Howard, "and he called the American Embassy in Lagos. A chartered plane was hastily dispatched to the grass airstrip."

Jack Howard and the rest of the crew flew to Lagos and waited for two more days while all the Port Harcourt evacuees straggled in. "I only know of two expatriates who were killed in the fighting," says Howard. "They were missionaries who had been captured in a remote village and were mistaken by the advancing troops for mercenary soldiers. The two missionaries were executed before the error was discovered."

Most of the evacuees in Lagos had no idea where their families had relocated. Many decided to head home on flights hastily arranged by their company. Howard decided to head for a company office in London. On arrival he learned from the office manager that his wife and children had spent the summer in Switzerland. A week earlier they had rented a flat in London. His ordeal was safely over.

Fernando's Hideaway

The Biafran resistance collapsed in January 1970, ending a tragic civil war that took many lives and ravaged the countryside. Howard did not return to Africa for another decade.

This time his destination was the small island of Equatorial Guinea, formerly known as Fernando Poo. Located 50 miles off the west coast of Africa, this little country was a '60s retreat for expatriates headed out for sun, beachcombing and peace and quiet.

But the tourist heyday was shortlived. In 1968, the island gained its independence from Spain and Francisco Macias Nguerma was elected president. The self-proclaimed president for life began a reign of terror that bankrupted his nation.

Plantation owners, teachers, small businessmen, clergy, just about anyone with education was arrested and thrown in prison. Some escaped, but many more were killed in this African gulag. Now the exploration vice president for a New York-based oil and gas company, Howard was assigned to research petroleum prospects there and Macias was being compared to Ugandan tyrant Idi Amin.

Howard had heard numerous stories about atrocities in Macias' prisons. After the country's economy ground to a halt, Macias asked the Russians for assistance. They were only too happy to oblige, and soon Equatorial Guinea was the sole Communist foothold in west Africa.

The reign of terror lasted all through the '70s and ended when Macias was overthrown in a military coup and shot in 1979. Reduced to a virtually illiterate country with overgrown cocoa plantations and depleted fishing grounds, the nation was eager to exploit potential oil fields in the surrounding territorial waters. "Oil was the only commodity the country had that might be of value," says Howard, "and it had the potential for bringing in much-needed foreign currency."

The delegation to Equatorial Guinea was comprised of two New York attorneys, one of whom was fluent in several languages, a black entrepreneur who convinced someone that he could open doors and move around in Third World countries better than whites, and Howard.

There was only one flight per week into Malabo, the capital, operated by Iberia Airlines. "We all wished later that we had missed the plane and gone home. Equatorial Guinea turned out to be a very dangerous and unpleasant place," Howard said later.

Most airport terminals in western Africa are very difficult. "There is generally little order or uniformity," says Howard. "Whoever pushes the hardest gets the best place in line. Compared to the terminal in Malabo, the other west African terminals operate with drill team precision."

The one-story, one-room metal building that served as a terminal had no windows, fans or flooring. The barely literate custom agent, a heavily armed officer and several lower ranking soldiers were on hand. Lines didn't exist. Everyone pushed and shoved, to get to the front and have his passport stamped and luggage cleared through customs. The heat and smell in the crowded room were overwhelming. Even though he was in the middle of over 100 people, it took Howard more than three hours to reach the custom agent.

At passport control passengers were told they needed four photographs. Howard had only two, and several of his companions had none. The soldiers grabbed the passports, dropped them in a bag and told the Americans to return when they had the necessary photos.

"Our Spanish-speaking attorney learned that a passport attorney was available in town. After walking a mile in the equatorial heat, we found the photo studio. It was an open-air building that consisted of an old iron chair, an African man with a Polaroid camera, and a line of 40 people. I never did find out why the government, such as it was, needed so many photos of its citizens. It probably had something to do with the near-total illiteracy of the population. Perhaps it was the only way of identifying people."

When he finally received his passport photos, Howard was horrified. He looked frustrated, worried and was covered with a mixture of red dust and sweat. This camera didn't lie.

"Clutching our valuable pictures we trudged back to the immigration office only to find it closed and deserted. Needless to say, we were concerned. We were in a foreign country that few people even knew existed. There was no U.S. consulate to help us, no way to communicate with home, and no passports to prove our identities. An hour later the passport control officer showed up. With papers in order we set off for our hotel."

The only hotel in town had 12 rooms that were completely booked. The manager explained that he had no reservations even though the team had a letter from the military governor saying they had confirmed accommodations. After a suitable bribe the manager recalled that someone would check out soon.

The room was wonderful, about 10 feet square with four army cots and an old wooden dresser. The cots were packed so tightly that the men could barely walk between them. "We had to stand on them to change clothes because there was so little room. Of course there was no air conditioning, but far worse, there were no screens on the windows, which made it easy for strange flying creatures to visit at night." Because there was no shower or bath, the visitors had to content themselves with sponge baths in the sink.

There was no argument about where to eat that night because the town had no restaurants. Everyone just went to bed hungry. The following morning the Americans headed to an open-air market for a makeshift breakfast. Suspecting that the bottled water had been filled from a spigot around the corner, Howard washed his food down with beer, which he also used to brush his teeth.

Unfortunately the bilingual attorney did drink the water and became violently ill. Because no doctor or hospital was available, his colleagues took him back to the airport, where he was put on a private plane for evacuation to the mainland. The black entrepreneur was supposed to accompany the attorney and then return to the island. "We never saw him again," says Howard. "The attorney made it back to Manhattan and insisted he would never leave New York."

The oilmen's difficulties in Equatorial Guinea were compounded by the fact that neither spoke Spanish. With considerable effort they hunted down government civil servants with a minimal command of English and explained their mission. In turn they were introduced to a military officer who was in charge of natural resources. He sounded suspicious, said he would check with his superiors and instructed the Americans to return in four days.

The men from the West killed time by exploring the streets of Malabo, a community that looked like an abandoned movie set. "It was totally unlike any of the west African towns I had ever seen. The streets were virtually empty; no visible commerce was taking place except at the open-air market. We could see people peeking at us from the dark interiors of their houses, but there was none of the noise or bustle that you would expect in this part of Africa. Everyone acted as though they were afraid to be seen in public. The many years of terror under the iron fist of Macias had taken a serious toll."

The pair found a local bar that prepared meals for regular customers. The fare was modest, but at least it was hot.

Finally, after four days in Malabo, their luck changed. A derrick barge working the Nigerian oil fields docked in Malabo for repairs. The Americans ran down to the dock and invited themselves aboard. The American captain said they could remain during his visit. The shared cabin was air conditioned, equipped with showers and decent food.

From this new base the men made their way through the bureaucracy, finally making contact with the right officials. After learning how to apply for a mineral concession, they realized nothing was going to happen on this first trip. Business moves slowly in the Third World and Malabo was no exception. On his last day in town Howard decided to shoot pictures. "I had been afraid to do so up to that point for fear that I would be thrown in jail or worse, but I now knew some government officials who presumably might assist me if I got in trouble. Besides, the officer in charge of the military garrison assured me that it would be all right to take pictures as long as I didn't photograph military buildings."

After walking around town, he spied an old church that looked like it would make a great shot. Unfortunately he didn't realize military barracks were in the background. As he was lining up to take the picture, an angry soldier charged Howard with a rifle equipped with a bayonet. The photographer backed up against a church door as the bayonet closed in on his chest. The soldier began shouting out questions in a Spanish dialect. He wanted the camera.

For 20 minutes Howard explained in a mixture of pidgin Spanish, English and sign language that the camera had family photos. Finally the soldier waved Howard off.

The following day an Iberia plane was scheduled to arrive in Malabo. It never showed up because there wasn't enough jet fuel in Malabo to supply it for the return trip. Most of the crowd drifted off. Howard and his colleague remained at the tiny terminal, hoping for a miracle. In mid-afternoon a small, single engine plane arrived from Douala, West Cameroon. The pilot agreed to take the two men back to the mainland for an outrageous fee. Thanks to quick connections they were back in New York the following day.

"This experience was without a doubt the worst business trip I have ever had the misfortune to take," says Howard. "We accomplished very little and were in mortal danger most of the time."

No Room for Anxiety

Indonesia can be a particularly challenging country for the business traveler who has seen everything. When the Intercontinental Hotel chain sent one of its managers to visit a Jakarta property, nothing seemed to go right. This hotel boss, who prefers to remain anonymous, flew to Indonesia from Australia on a stomach churning flight. But once she reached the airport terminal, it was obvious the plane was less threatening than her destination. People swarmed around her, and it was unbearably humid: "I wandered aimlessly until I saw a sign being held up with my name on it. The manager of the Jakarta Intercontinental escorted me the rest of the way to the hotel. I was sick with culture shock and during the ride through the city beggars swarmed the car. A woman thrust her baby at me through the window and when I saw her face I noticed blood oozing from her mouth. Not until later did I realize that the 'blood' came from the juice of the beetlenut fruit.

"When we arrived at the hotel I lay on my bed and fell asleep. As I woke in the dark room I realized that the knob to my door was turning. Someone had a key to my room and was trying to get in. I yelled 'go away, stay out' and the door

quickly shut. I rationalized that it was a mistake and that someone had tried to open the wrong room. The second time the
knob turned I knew it wasn't a weird coincidence. I lay awake
listening for the rest of the night, terrified to leave my room.
Towards the end of the night I began writing the longest letter I had ever written to my mother."

The Spice Guy

As director of spice procurement for McCormick and Company, Hank Kaestner has spent 30 years traveling the globe
sourcing raw materials. On 139 trips he has had his share of
disasters and close calls. In Madagascar, the world's largest
supplier of vanilla, Kaestner had to take a three hour Cessna
flight to Antalaha. Enroute to the center of the nation's vanilla
region he was told that the village chief was going to offer him
the youngest, prettiest virgin. Refusing this gift would be a
serious breach of etiquette and could threaten the crucial business relationship between the vanilla producers and his company, number one in the vanilla business. By the time the plane
touched down in Antalaha, Kaestner, a family man, was in a
panic. Only after meeting his hosts did he learn, to his relief,
that the vanilla virgin custom had ended years earlier.

On another trip, after a long work week in Singapore, Kaestner decided to take a train to Taman Negara Park in the
Malaysian jungle. When the weekend excursion ended he
boarded a train back down the Malay peninsula to Singapore
and fell asleep. There was no way he could miss his final stop
because Singapore was the end of the line. The following morning he awoke to find himself alone in the train. The cars had
been parked in a yard and his fellow passengers had all disembarked. "I was alone. I looked out of the window, and in
the distance could see the station." But when he entered the

terminal to hail a cab, Kaestner realized something was wrong. This was definitely not the right terminal. During the night he had been sleeping so soundly, he missed a transfer and wound up in Kuala Lumpur, Malaysia. "It's the only time I didn't know which country I was in."

Another time, in Belem, at the mouth of the Brazilian Amazon, Kaestner visited a pepper plantation. Access by light plane took a mere two hours. After a five-hour walking tour, he returned from the hot, humid plantation to the town of Tome Acu where the only cold beverage was a local beer called Antarctica. The 29-year-old Kaestner downed several, but the pilot didn't limit himself. While Kaestner was on the walking tour, the pilot had stayed at the bar and gotten himself pleasantly drunk.

Clearly it was time for a management decision. Kaestner could get into the plane with a drunken pilot or take a two-day cruise down the malaria-infested Amazon to Belem. He chose the plane, figuring that the pilot could probably take off without much trouble and by arrival time in Belem two hours later would be sober enough to land.

Takeoff went well and, as the plane turned toward Belem, a thunderstorm loomed ahead. Kaestner wanted to return to Tome Acu and wait for the storm to pass, but he couldn't because the pilot was too drunk to land. "I had heard stories of light planes being caught in thunderstorm updrafts, and being elevated to 40,000 feet where oxygen is so scarce that death is inevitable. What a way to die, I thought," The storm moved closer to the plane, until, at the last minute, the cloud parted just a bit. Visible in the bright sunlight on the other side was Belem. The pilot threaded his way through the opening and landed without incident. By then he had sobered up.

The Heat Was On

Sometimes bedding down in a strange country can be a challenge, particularly when you can travel in areas where first class accommodations are heavily booked. Visiting Hyderabad, India, to meet with government officials and commercial electronics firms, one California businessman had a hard time beating the heat. "The temperature was unbearably hot. I could never figure out how hot … since it was centigrade." At the time of his visit the only available lodging was at the former home of a ruling prince. Unfortunately this maharaja's residence had been converted to a hotel without air conditioning.

"During the night, it became unbearable and I had trouble breathing in the hot, humid weather. Since I was on the second floor, I looked out the window to see a roof just below my window. I moved the mattress out on the sloping roof to get some air and sleep. I had just fallen asleep when I woke up with two iguanas walking around on my back."

In Frankfurt, Germany, the same traveler had the opposite problem. He made the mistake of checking into an airport hotel with a broken heater in the middle of a very cold winter. No one at the front desk was able to remedy the problem. Freezing, he got up, dressed and went downstairs for extra blankets. By now no one was even on duty. He returned to his room, grabbed a mattress, folded it in half and shoved it between the front door and an outer privacy door. Because the space was narrow, the mattress curled up on both ends into a U shape. Since the bathroom entrance was located between these two doors, he turned on the shower to create steam. He wound up with an hour of steam and sleep in his makeshift U bed.

This American had better luck during a winter trip to Chelmsford, Britain. Arriving during a time of energy conservation, he felt like he was checking in to a refrigerated meat locker. The spring loaded electric heater was set to click off moments after it began producing any power. He spent two hours rigging a series of pillow covers together that tied down the heater control knobs down to the floor. "It kept the heater on. I got two hours of sleep that night."

Know Your Worth

Dr. Dennis J. O'Neill of Chappaqua, New York, finds Caracas' warm climate a pleasure compared to winters in the Northeast but many aspects of visiting there 13 times over five years offset that enjoyment.

"I will never forget my first trip. It was just after a promotion to a new job that offered international travel. My travel-worn colleague, whose mother was Venezuelan, rested through the nine-hour flight when we were to fill in our visa paper; the tiny form offered three options (business, pleasure and something else). Feeling competent to make this trivial decision during my colleague's nap and knowing that an inspection of my luggage would reveal the accouterments of a business — as opposed to a pleasure — trip, I checked the 'Business' box and tucked it away with my passport."

Venezuela's Simon Bolivar Airport was exciting — particularly the "customs" official packing a machine gun that he used as both a threat and a crutch. "He looked at my form and told me I would have to take the plane back to New York because my papers were not in order. My colleague swung into very animated action. With arms flailing he spoke in Spanish that I could not understand.

"When a piece of paper dropped from my colleague's pants pocket, yelling stopped as the customs agent picked it up, motioned to me, grabbed my visa form, put a bigger check mark in the 'Pleasure' box, smiled and said, 'Welcome to Venezuela.'

"Are you going to tell me what just happened? I asked my colleague.

"'The customs guy thought that you are worth a hundred bucks.'

"What did you tell him I am worth?

"'Fifty,'" he said.

"I walked a little more before I asked him, For the record, what am I worth?

"'Fifty.'"

Water, Water Everywhere

The Taminaco was considered the only place to stay on business trips to Caracas. In fact, it was said to be the finest hotel in all of Venezuela. During a moment of relaxing by the pool after having a bout of diarrhea, O'Neill watched a young hotel employee carrying a plastic rack containing maybe 20 empty bottles of the local bottled water as he emerged from the kitchen's back door. He came around the side of the swimming pool and disappeared. "I got up to follow him from a discreet distance. I watched him fill the bottled water bottles from a hose, press on crown caps, and take them back into the kitchen door. I immediately switched to beer, and it is not so bad to brush your teeth with."

Cerveza!

Speaking of beer, on one evening without business commitments, O'Neill was drawn to the festive outdoor grill at the hotel. He walked up to the bar to use his one word of Spanish: Cerveza!

"My beer arrived and after a few sips, I noticed a mid-50s

looking gentleman sitting at the bar with a younger man, per-haps his son, standing next to him. We said hello and the young man asked if I was German. I felt some small triumph in think-ing that I was not screamingly American, perhaps "a citizen of the world." The young man translated and he asked me what I did for a living. I explained that I was a management consultant and he asked me if that was something like being a teacher. I said it was a little like that. The translation went back to the older gentleman and the younger one translated for me: "My friend would like to know if you would like to join us in our room and you can teach us everything you know."

3

Air Travel: Up Up and Oy Vey

ONE OF THE AIRLINES' most impressive antidotes for "descent anxiety" is an inflight mapping system that gives passengers the security of knowing their exact position, heading, airspeed and time to their destination. Among the carriers featuring this system is Northwest Airlines. Minute by minute passengers can see their position and routing thanks to a direct link to the plane's navigation system. Offering instant updates and noting cities and landmarks enroute, the display works as a kind of a video security blanket.

Unfortunately for Joe Carr and 240 other passengers aboard a Northwest DC-10 bound from Detroit to Frankfurt, Germany, the electronic map was not visible to the three people on the plane who really needed it—the pilot, first officer and flight engineer. As director of machine technology for Johnson Controls, Carr averaged 17 trips a year to Europe. While this particular flight in September 1995 seemed routine, there was one serious problem. In Shannon, Ireland, a controller accidentally switched Flight 52's destination from Frankfurt to Brussels, Belgium, 200 miles away.

The error was compounded by the fact that the air traffic system in other European countries accepted this erroneous flight plan and kept the jet on the wrong course. Had they walked into the passenger compartment and looked at the electronic map display, any of the experienced flight crew could have easily seen what was obvious to everyone else aboard— the plane was headed to the wrong airport. Up in the galley the flight attendants were talking nervously about the navigational error. They elected not to inform the crew because airline policy prevents them from interrupting the pilots during approach unless there is a cabin emergency.

The passengers were feeling nervous, too.

"Pilots and flight engineers are supposed to know their location," says Carr. "Incredibly, the pilot called in to the tower, assuming he was in Germany. His repeated calls to the 'Frankfurt tower' actually went to the Brussels tower where controllers assigned a runway and guided him in. Apparently he didn't know he was dealing with Belgian controllers. Only when the plane broke through the cloud cover did it become obvious from the landscape that the plane wasn't in Germany."

The flight attendants looked out the window trying to figure out what was wrong without alarming passengers. Some were concerned that this unannounced destination change signaled a hijacking. Finally, the pilot came on with one of the more interesting arrival announcements in the history of commercial aviation:

"Ladies and gentlemen, this is your pilot. We have a very embarrassing situation. Those of you who travel to Frankfurt know that we aren't there. We've mistakenly landed in Brussels." Carr got off the plane and caught a Sabena flight to Berlin. But most of his fellow passengers waited on the ground for six hours until a relief crew took the plane to Germany. The pilot, who had a perfect record, the first officer and engineer were all grounded while the mistake was investigated.

"I have never seen a crew led down a primrose path like

this one was," a federal aviation official said after the landing. Flight 52 is now a textbook case taught in human factors courses. Joe Carr believes that under the circumstances, the pilot "did the right thing. He went ahead and landed the plane." Carr and the rest of the passengers received 5,000 World Perks frequent flyer miles for their inconvenience.

It's Awfully Quiet in the Cockpit

Have you ever wondered what pilots are really doing when the plane is in the air? Are they passing around the Cherry Coke, on the phone to the massage parlor for an appointment or perhaps just busy putting their papers in order for an IRS audit? Everyone knows, or at least believes in their heart, that in this automated world the planes fly themselves. According to a director of flight safety for Indian Airlines, pilots should do transcendental meditation before a downwind landing. In his professional journal article "Human Factors in Identifying and Handling Tail-Wind Landing Problems," Captain B.K. Bhasin emphasized the "tranquility factor." He suggests that it is important for the pilot to "regulate the dwelling habit of mind, i.e., turn your face away when you sense that observational quality is changing to yearning."

Don't get me wrong. I don't have anything against Capt. Bhasin's suggestion that pilots use diaphragmatic breathing and "allow the air to be inhaled softly, slowly and deeply so that it can be felt to the navel." But I think before boarding this carrier I would like to know at what point the pilot comes out of TM. On second thought, maybe I'll just take another airline.

Delightful Snafus

One of the great things about business travel snafus is they often make great stories that delight friends and colleagues at parties, business gatherings or just about any social occasion. Jack Branagh, who travels extensively to visit his real estate interests, is always a hit with his story about the day he had to evacuate a flight shortly after landing in Wichita, Kansas. Smoke was pouring into the cabin and the slides were down. "Just a minute," Branagh of Oakland, California, insisted as he tried to pull his American Express card out of the Air Phone slot. The card wouldn't budge and the call was in progress. The flight attendants insisted and Branagh tugged again as he visualized the inevitable $4,000 bill from American Express. Finally he had to give up and slide down the chute like everyone else. "Fortunately, somehow, in the crisis, the phone shut down. But that was one scary phone call."

Branagh travels a good deal to France, where he has property interests in the Bordeaux region. He completed one trip, only to find on checking in for his return flight to San Francisco that he was traveling on his wife Lynn's passport. "My wife is very feminine and we do not look at all alike," says Branagh. "The customs and airport officials in San Francisco and Paris just waved me through on the outbound trip. But when I went to the United counter for my flight home, they caught the discrepancy." After more than an hour of intense conversation with customs officials in Paris, the airline let Branagh board.

"I just told them I had grabbed my wife's passport in haste and they bought the story. The real problem was San Francisco. The customs officer gave me a very wide-eyed look when I told him what had happened. He just knew something was up but was very cool about it. The whole thing was treated as our little secret. 'Now if anyone asks you,' he told me with a wink, 'it was your wife who made this trip, not you. Do you understand?'" Is it any wonder some of his friends now call him Jacqueline?

The Russian Connection

International business consultant Fred Hornbruch had two
options when he headed off to Volgograd in southern Russia.
He could fly Aeroflot or he could walk. Sounds like a no-brainer?
Maybe not. Hornbruch, part of a productivity enhancement
consultant group sponsored by the federal government, was
thoroughly soaked as he disembarked from his Frankfurt-
Moscow flight. The lack of jetways or covered walkways was
only the first of a series of anomalies he discovered in the Soviet
air transit system. After shuttling across Moscow to a small
domestic airport for the trip to Volgograd, he learned that
there would be an airline charge for excess luggage. Or, the
helpful agent explained, he could win a considerable discount
by simply paying cash.

Boarding the packed flight, Hornbruch noticed a few housekeeping problems. The carpeting was loose, there were no
headrests and hand luggage normally stowed under seats or
in overhead bins was stacked up in the aisle. A friendly Saint
Bernard and a cat were exploring the cabin as the American
noticed that window seat passengers were bending inward to
avoid hitting the curved fuselage.

The American consultant heard a commotion near the
front of the plane. It was the flight crew, including the captain
bearing a bottle of Jack Daniels. From his seat, Hornbruch
could hear the reason why the plane wasn't moving. The pilots
and the flight attendants were having an impromptu party in
the cockpit.

The flight to Volgograd was uneventful for Hornbruch,
who declined both the mystery meat and an opportunity to
buy a lottery ticket from his flight attendant. After the plane
docked, passengers rose to disembark. The flight attendants

began shouting for them to sit down. "Everyone sat silently," says Hornbruch, "as the flight crew, emerging from the cockpit where they had obviously been drinking and smoking during the flight, got off first."

The return trip to Moscow was easier, but transferring to another airport for a flight to Leningrad took over three hours. "We were delayed because of traffic tieups relating to the shutdown of the Duma (parliament)." All the city police chiefs were meeting to decide which leader they wanted to support, ultimately settling on Boris Yeltsin. "We got a good look at the tanks and troops lined up outside the Duma," says Hornbruch. "Not a bad history lesson."

Can't Beat that Security

Personally, I yearn for the old days of air travel when people just went to the airport, boarded planes and took off. There were no X-ray machines, no embarrassing questions about who packed your suitcase and no need to show your driver's license at check-in. From Israel, where pat-down searches and interviews are done by military trained security guards, to the Philippines where security goes the limit, air travel is a constant reminder that anything can happen. It's hard to believe that once upon a time Manila's Ninoy Aquino International terminal was on the Federal Aviation Administration's blacklist for inadequate security. Now it's a model for airport managers everywhere. Probably the only international airport named for a politician assassinated on the premises (Aquino lived for only about 20 seconds after deplaning on his final, tragic return to the Philippines in 1983), this terminal has security second only to the Nevada Test Site.

Most impressive is the comprehensive approach to passenger safety. Many airports around the world have sophisticated equipment that can detect the presence of weapons and explosives. But most lack rudimentary screening at the front door. Guards are poorly paid and often unarmed. Hand searches and pat-downs range from rare to nonexistent. And once you clear the X-ray/metal-detector check, there's little additional scrutiny.

Compare this with Manila's fail-safe approach. Non-passengers here to greet arriving passengers must purchase tickets that allow them to stand in a contained waiting gallery just inside the front door. Only passengers holding tickets are allowed beyond this point. From here they must proceed through one of the best defensive lines this side of the National Football League.

If you count customs and passport control, there are seven security checks between the curb and the plane. All luggage is X-rayed before you can even approach customs and the ticket counter. After checking in for a flight, passengers must head through immigration and passport control to reach the departure area. While these precautions would be sufficient for most airports, they are only a warm-up here.

A second set of X-ray machines and metal detectors is on hand to reinspect all passengers and their carry-ons. In addition, many items are individually searched. Every passenger is subjected to a thorough body search. Finally, and this is the part I like the best, each ticket holder's name is checked off as he hands over his boarding pass to the agent. If anyone checks in luggage and then fails to show for the flight, departure is held up to allow removal of the baggage from the aircraft.

There's more. Armed guards are posted at aircraft staircases, inside jetways leading to aircraft, on the tarmac next to the plane and even at baggage claim areas. While many of these precautions are taken at foreign airports around the world, I've never seen so many checkpoints.

Many American terminals could obviously benefit by incorporating some of these precautions into their own security systems. Though passenger safety is clearly a primary concern, Ninoy Aquino International does not make passengers feel like they are on an Alcatraz tour. In fact, this airport has a number of amenities other terminals would do well to duplicate.

Just beyond the boarding area, as you head for immigration, there's a free public phone available to any passenger who has to make a last-minute local call. Also here is a very convenient copying service. And there's no need to visit a restaurant to get service. In the passenger lounge area, waiters and waitresses obligingly take your order for anything from a scotch on the rocks to a mango shake with a chicken sandwich. Quality is fine and, unlike many airport concessions around the world, prices are reasonable.

At the antique store, worry beads are purchased by passengers concerned about cargo doors and plastic explosives. Some have, no doubt, even stopped off across from the Aquino Airport to pray at Our Lady of the Airwaves, a church with a stainless steel propeller attached to the bell tower.

Although nothing can take all the worry out of flying, it's nice to know that when you do land in Manila, someone has come up with a system to protect you and your luggage. Unlike many terminals, no one gets out of the baggage area until they produce the necessary luggage claim checks. When you climb into a cab, the dispatcher hands you a receipt for all luggage. At your destination, you must sign a form acknowledging receipt of all luggage. There's additional baggage screening and a metal detector at the entrance to your hotel.

There are good reasons for all this security. Michael Klyszeiko of Read-Rite Corporation tells of an aquaintance who came to Manila in 1996 without realizing how corrupt and dangerous the city can be. Leaving a facility one evening he decided to take a cab rather than the recommended company shuttle bus. Several minutes into the cab ride he realized that he was not being taken back to the hotel. Instead he was driven to a remote area, where he was beaten and robbed by the cab driver and his gang. Then the driver courteously took the man to his destination. He returned home to the United States the next day.

The Missing Suitcase

For many travelers, the most frightening part of their trip is standing at the end of the baggage carousel waiting for belongings. A friend of mine, determined to find a missing suitcase in Rome, insisted on visiting the Alitalia lost-luggage facility. A guard opened the door and she suddenly found herself in a giant warehouse with thousands upon thousands of pieces of luggage separated from their owners. "If I had a month," she told me, "there would have been no way to track my bag down."

The airlines do, of course, work hard to reunite passengers with their missing luggage. Clarice Cohen of Milwaukee took a three-week trip around Israel while her missing bag languished in the Tel Aviv Airport. El Al returned it two months later. Everything was fine until she opened the suitcase.

Missing were two tape recorders, 26 rolls of film, a pair of shoes, socks, a sweater, cigars and makeup. Everything else was ruined by bottles of shampoo and conditioner that had spilled open. That was strange because she didn't use that brand.

Ideally it would be best to travel only with goods you can afford to lose. This isn't possible for business travelers like Frank Christopher, an award-winning documentary filmmaker living in Southern California. His trouble started when he and a four-person team arrived at the Nairobi Airport to begin working on an Agency for International Development film documenting Columbia University public health projects in Rwanda, the Ivory Coast and Nigeria. None of their 29 pieces of luggage, including personal belongings and $60,000 worth of video equipment, arrived. Instead of flying off to Rwanda as scheduled the following day, the group remained at a Nairobi hotel for four days sorting out the problem via telex and phone.

The bags, which had failed to make his team's flight from New York to Rome, were stranded at Kennedy Airport. After they were finally traced, all 29 pieces were sent to Rome. "But when we showed up at the Nairobi Airport to meet a connecting Air Kenya flight," recalls Christopher, "only 24 bags arrived.

"Losing luggage is a nightmare. But it's even worse when the bags are separated because you start thinking you've been ripped off. Adding to my suspicion was the fact that the missing bags contained $10,000 worth of tripods, video monitors and test equipment. Pan Am insisted that it was someone else's fault, so we were back to square one with the meter ticking on crew time in excess of $1,000 a day, plus hotel bills.

"Already a week behind on our tight schedule, three crew members and I left for Rwanda to work without the missing equipment. We were unable to get steady zooms or review what we'd shot. If there was a problem, we couldn't do anything about it. Of course, in Rwanda there was no Sony technician around to fix things.

"Air Kenya insisted they only picked up 24 pieces in Rome. Pan Am suggested someone had ripped off the remaining five bags in Italy. Although we carried special insurance on the equipment, we couldn't process a claim for the missing bags until they were declared lost. We went ahead and ordered new equipment."

Frustrated and getting the run-around 12 days after he left New York, Christopher took his problem to the dean of Columbia's School of Public Health. This man got action with a call to the chairman of Pan Am. It turned out that the last five bags had been separated from the shipment in Rome and returned to Kennedy, where they were being held at customs. Finally, after two weeks, the missing equipment reached the crew.

Having lost more than $10,000 on hotel bills, telexes and long-distance calls by this point, Christopher's crew became very protective: "As we traveled through Africa, we insisted on being allowed onto the tarmac to count the luggage being loaded onto the plane. During a stopover in Lagos, an airport notorious for theft, we actually got off the plane to watch the unloading. Sure enough, they started taking off two of our bags. We screamed and hollered to make sure they got back on the continuation of our flight to the Ivory Coast."

The Long Delay

One of the worst features of long trips is the way unexpected delays can turn minor problems into big ones. Linda Petersen, a music educator living in Milwaukee, took off from Los Angeles on the second leg of a trip home from Australia when she noticed that the plane was climbing slowly. The pilot announced that he was jettisoning fuel and heading back to the airport. Unable to get another flight back to Wisconsin, she flew to Chicago and rented a car for the drive home. When she reached her driveway, Petersen realized that a key ring with her house and car keys were checked with the attendant at the parking lot next to the Milwaukee airport. She headed back to the lot on the frigid winter night and found the attendant asleep in his office. "I pounded on the door. I yelled. I threw stones. I cried. Finally, I walked to the neighboring parking ramp and asked the attendant if I could use their phone. He obliged. I telephoned. The guy still did not wake up. The nice man from the neighboring parking ramp walked back with me, and used a flashlight and plenty of noise to awaken the comatose parking attendant. He gave me my car keys, drove the rental car back and I went home—about 38 hours after leaving Sydney. I've never given my house keys to a parking attendant since."

Let Them Eat Cake

There are times when passengers just can't take it any more. Flight delays can lead to all sorts of complications. Lorraine Battle, a California food stylist, boarded an early morning San Francisco flight to Atlanta, never imagining a cake she had brought aboard for a friend would become the centerpiece of an inflight food fight. After an hour in the air, engine trouble forced the pilot to turn the flight around and head back to San Francisco. Because the flight left at the crack of dawn many of the passengers hadn't eaten breakfast. When the meal service was canceled due to the sudden decision to return to California, one of the passengers suggested trying Battle's cake. Before she could react, someone popped up and went for the overhead bin. Battle jumped up and began guarding her cake. After heavy negotiation, it became clear that the hungry passengers weren't kidding. "Things were getting hot and heavy and we brought down the cake," says a friend along for the ride. "They let us keep half and gobbled up the rest."

Travel Daze

It's no secret that people sitting next to each other on a plane can be paying vastly different fares depending on when they bought their ticket and where they are going. Often it's the business traveler heading out on short notice or making a multicity trip who bears the brunt of this economic discrimination in the era of so-called deregulation. I remember sitting on a one hour flight from Minneapolis to Michigan with a man who had paid over $700 for a short-notice ticket, more than double the cost of a cross-country journey on the same airline for passengers who could book ahead. Why would the airlines elect to punish passengers helping fill empty seats at the last minute?

The airlines have created a fare rule book that isn't even written down. Fares, conditions of sale, tariff rules, itinerary requirements, length of stay requirements, age requirements, discounts, change fees—every one of these conditions can be altered with little or no warning. Your guess is as good as mine on the probability of today's bargain fare being available tomorrow. Some of the best fares aren't revealed unless you ask about them. And even when the fares aren't changing, the deals are so complicated you can never be sure what a ticket calls for. I have called two agents for the same airline within five minutes of each other for a price on an identical itinerary and received quotes $100 apart.

Often the terms and conditions are so complicated that questions on fine points, such as changing a reservation for medical reasons, have to be referred to an airline referee sitting on the "fare desk." Acting as judge and jury, they actually rule on whether or not a purchased ticket can be altered, reissued, credited or refunded. For example, if you are going to your aunt's funeral they might give you a discount if you give them information on the funeral home and the name of the mortician.

Of course the airlines do a pretty good job of not letting the public know that these bereavement fares even exist. I found out about this from a fellow train passenger headed from Los Angeles to Chicago for his grandmother's funeral. All the carriers, including budget airlines, quoted him a $1,500 price for a quick trip to Chicago for the services. When I mentioned that he could have found a last minute bereavement fare close to the price of his $230 Amtrak roundtrip he confessed surprise.

Regarding the tendency of many airlines to overcharge people who can't plan ahead, Northwest Airlines wanted $435 for an instant-purchase flight from Muskegon, Michigan, to Detroit, a 180-mile trip. This was more than the cost of a ticket from Michigan to Europe bought a few weeks in advance.

Multicity travel is another nightmare. If your itinerary includes more than two stops, look out. When I tried to book a trip from San Francisco to Albuquerque, Detroit, New York and Hartford, Connecticut, my travel agent refused to even quote the price. It turns out that it would have been cheaper to buy an around the world ticket than to visit this handful of American cities. There was only one economical way out. I rode Amtrak on the New Mexico-Michigan leg of the trip.

A Poetic Problem

Sometimes a travel experience can reduce you to babbling. Other times it can bring out a literary form you probably never knew you were capable of. Read the experience of Valerie Lewis, of Hicklebee's a San Jose, California, children's bookstore, who was traveling to teach a class on bookselling in another land, far, far away.

> Flying to Latvia
> United Air ... International terminal: Sat A.M.
> Wait in line.
> Wrong terminal

Run to the right one.

Wait in line.

Get just the seat I want & now it's all worth it.

Plane departs on time (11:00 A.M.).

Relax.

Pilot announces plane must return due to problems
with left engine.

Passengers remain in plane for 45 minutes more.

I'm thankful for the 2 hrs & 45 minute scheduled wait in
NY before my flight to Frankfurt.

There I will meet Tracy with the red moustache.

He will recognize me by my book, *The Baltic Revolution:
Estonia, Latvia, Lithuania and the Path to
Independence . . .*

We'll travel together to Frankfurt, then on to Riga where
we will meet our Latvian colleagues and set off for a
small city.

Plane departs after 45 minutes.

Pilot announces plane must return due to mechanical
problems.

Passengers wait.

Pilot announces it will be another 30 minutes.

It is now 1:00

Stress level begins to rise.

Even if we take off by 1:30, that allows only 15 minutes to
make my next flight.

Woman passenger who apparently collects lead BBs,
drops them on my foot while attempting to place
them on the bin above me.

She screams for ice in dismay at my apparent pain.

She needs to go back to her seat.

I smile and say all is fine.

She insists.
I win.
She is gone.
My foot is throbbing.
I wait a long five minutes before carefully slipping off
    my shoe to observe damage.
She is back ... screaming for ice.
My stress level rises.
I assure her I am fine & only had an itch.
It is 1:30.
I take my carry-on luggage out of the overhead and
    limp to the front of the plane.
I'm getting off.
The flight attendant disagrees: polite but firm.
Pilot announces the plane is out of commission.
I fly off the plane.
United Airlines desk.
I must get to Frankfurt.
Emergency change of plans (planes).
Chicago, not New York.
I have 10 minutes before the flight to Chicago leaves.
Race to the gate.
Huff & puff.
Last one on plane.
Steward sympathetic.
Plane takes off.
Stays in air.
I suddenly realize my itinerary is with teaching
    materials in my luggage on ill plane.
I don't know my final destination.
It's somewhere in Latvia.
Not Riga.

I don't know who is meeting me.

It's someone in Latvia.

I call my neighbor, Merry, from the seat behind.

She goes to my house & tries to find names & numbers on my desk.

She finds a name that appears Latvian, but not a city.

Her voice is spent.

Good luck.

It is imperative I make my flight to Frankfurt for last chance to meet with colleagues.

Steward doesn't think there will be a problem.

I maintain the same degree of stress.

High.

20 minutes prior to landing, steward asks for my ticket to show the pilot.

He's sorry.

I may not make my next flight.

Trade winds.

Stress level soars.

Plane lands.

15 minutes before Frankfurt bound plane's scheduled departure.

I'm allowed to be first one off plane.

Race.

Board United to Frankfurt seconds before doors closed.

I see that Andy is on board. He's from Chicago.

Stress level drops.

In the middle seat. It's ok. I made it. Andy's on the plane. Phew!

Flight attendant finds me an aisle.

Relieved, I go into the bathroom.

Stretch, reach, bend. Laugh at my plight.

Glasses fall from my head into toilet.
Decision.
Retrieve glasses.
Return to my seat.
My luggage is somewhere.
Land in Frankfurt.
Armored vehicles & guards with semi automatics.
Andy & I have 2½ hours before flight to Riga.
We talk.
$4.00 Cokes.
Go to terminal to Riga.
Meet Stan & Tracy with the red moustache.
They all have tickets to Riga.
I don't.
All my flights were canceled.
And no luggage.
No wonder it's called terminal.
I get another ticket to Riga.
Flight's leaving in 10 minutes.
Andy joins me in four hall run to customer service for
    return tickets to USA.
Almost miss plane to Riga.
Wait-listed to Boston. My canceled tickets are no longer
    available.
In Riga, Anara takes me to Lufthansa desk to sort out
    ticket & luggage problems.
Secure ticket from Frankfurt to Boston.
Am still wait-listed to San Francisco from Boston.
Computer crashes.
They'll do their best.
On to Conference center & wondrous days of traveling
    & teaching.

Luggage arrives three days later.
Thrilled!
Time for journey home.
Riga to Frankfurt.
Fine.
In Frankfurt I find I have tickets all the way through.
Relief!
Flying with Stan.
Fun.
Tired.
An hour before landing stewardess comments on how
    close my connection is to SF.
After all, I'll have to go through customs.
With only an hour.
No problem, I think.
Turbulence.
Major turbulence.
Hit "the storm" hurricane trailings.
More turbulence.
Pilot is sorry, but we'll land late because storm has
    affected all flights.
Stress level rises.
No sleep since sometime yesterday.
Stan helps, but luggage takes too long.
I rush out into the rain pushing luggage cart,
    demanding location of terminal C.
Take the bus I'm advised.
No time. Ten minutes only. Again.
I charge into terminal C, mascara dripping off my chin,
    nostrils heaving, soaking.
Rain drenched bag lady.
Last on the plane, all bodies retracting into their seats

Away from my storm-soaked march.
United we do not stand. Against all odds.
United flew.
And I, in its bowels, made it home.

4

Trade Shows: Strictly Unconventional

ACROSS AMERICA, city officials are trying to pay off bond issues by bringing business people to vast, unmanageable, over-crowded, poorly ventilated, badly catered convention centers. So who said the world was perfect? Trade shows and conventions are vital to making sales, establishing contacts and rubbing shoulders with others in business. And some of the foibles are downright entertaining.

Every step of the way, the travel industry seems to be conspiring against the conventioneer. Airlines insist that your trip include a Saturday stay if you want to avoid paying two or three times the normal fare. Cities impose outrageous taxes on rental cars that hit up to 28% (in Seattle), to cover the cost of building new football stadiums (Detroit) and other exasperating forms of corporate welfare. Hotels on convention bus routes have been known to offer "special" rates that are much higher than normal. Security can also be a problem when your goods are delivered to foreign conventions by certain freight forwarders who have special techniques for maximizing their bottom line at your expense.

Location, Location, Location

One of the most tortuous aspects of convention life is simply getting to events. For unknown reasons, most trade shows are in crowded cities rather than lovely resorts or beautiful college towns. I've never been able to figure this out. It seems to me that the ideal location would be Vail, Santa Fe, Maui, the Catskills, Ann Arbor, Colonial Williamsburg or Napa Valley. Many of these areas have large hotels and a simple shuttle bus system that would make it easy to move between a variety of venues. Cruise ships might also work well. You could just line several up in a pleasant harbor like Key West and have a ball. Especially at sunset.

Instead, conventions are in improbable places like New York, where cross-town traffic, a fact of life for anyone who has to reach the Javits Center on the west side of Manhattan, creates a kind of hysteria that is typical in the business world. In one instance a bike race made it impossible for conventioneers to cross 9th Street enroute to the New York convention center for the National Stationery Show. When we did bravely step into the street, bikes veered and tumbled, sending riders careening into one another in an only-in-New York moment.

Hail, Hail

Monica Holmes, who co-owns Hicklebee's children's bookstore in San Jose, tells this story about a day at the Javits Center. She hailed a cab to a party in Greenwich Village with two business partners, her sister Valerie Lewis (of Latvia fame from Chapter 3), and Jan Gottlieb, as well as Niki Salan, owner of Cover to Cover, a San Francisco bookstore.

"Driving a cab in New York must be very stressful," Monica

said as their driver took out a knife and put it on the dashboard. With one hand on a tire iron and the other on the wheel, he floored the accelerator in hot pursuit of a limo. The limo driver had made the mistake of tossing a cup of ice at their cab driver (in retaliation for being cut off in traffic) and the Californians were treated to an unforgettable New York taxi experience—a 10-minute high speed chase uptown, downtown, cross town, under bridges, horns blasting. As Manhattan zipped past their window, Monica, who appeared to be in shock, glanced down at the tire iron between her and the driver.

"You know in California," she said, "when we get in stressful situations like this we take deep breaths, lots of deep breaths. You might want to try that."

The driver, by now completely postal, cursed loudly.

"That's right," said Monica, "deep breathing is really helpful when you're feeling upset."

After the limo finally escaped, the driver headed down to the village charging the party for the entire extra chase time and mileage as if it had been some kind of thrill ride. The passengers didn't haggle. They just wanted out. Heading toward the party Jan turned to Valerie and asked: "Where's Monica?"

She had disappeared. A minute later Monica ran up breathless. "Sorry, it just took me forever to find the money for a tip."

Dead to Rights

In November 1992 I was representing my employer, a travel guidebook publisher, at the Frankfurt Book Fair in Germany. This was my second Frankfurt Show. The first had gone great thanks to the sale of French rights to six books to a Canadian publisher. Unfortunately the second year was less exciting. With roughly 7,000 booths and 250,000 people in attendance, the Frankfurt *Buchmesse* is an event that many publishers go out of their way to avoid. I remember at my first show mentioning to one of the employees at the huge trade show hall about the horror of an editor dropping dead in the very crowded agents center.

"What a shame," I said as the claxon horn of an ambulance blared on the plaza below us.

"That's only the first one we've lost at this show," she told me. "We lose a lot more at the auto show."

Not All Wet after All

The sheer congestion at Frankfurt creates a rush hour that lasts five days. European publishers, who co-print their books in half a dozen languages, rely on this fair to set up much of their rights business for the coming year. As a newcomer I made the mistake of focusing on selling German rights to our American travel books. The Germans, who appear to enjoy more vacation time than the rest of the world put together, are never short of guide books and, I discovered to my dismay, that there are so many good German guide book publishers few of them are seriously interested in buying American rights.

As I was being rejected and stood up right and left, I noticed, out of the corner of my eye, a book across the aisle that was all wet. Actually there was water inside plastic sleeves glued to die cut pages. Each of the water windows contained plastic fish that swam around when you shook the book. Neat idea, and American rights were available. But when I got home my publisher said no. "I can't believe he turned it down," one of my colleagues told me. The next day I was on the phone to Nature Company. They ordered 5,000 copies and RDR Books was in business.

One reason trade shows are so well attended is that they

bring together such beginners with large companies searching for new ideas. A friend of mine who has developed technology that can convert text to speech in English and foreign languages found his biggest customer by accident at a West Coast show. It was here that one company, who could not use his product, recommended him to another vendor who bought the concept immediately. Sales soared and years later the business was sold for more than $15 million.

Thinking Small

In my own case it would have been difficult to start a business without trade shows. Despite all the complaints, these shows remain a launching pad for businesses of all kinds. While these events can be stressful and frustrating, the fact remains that they are a necessity for any business.

These shows also underscore something that is obvious to just about everyone out there in the business world. Although it seldom enjoys the publicity it deserves, small business is the most important economic force of the late 20th century.

In the United States small businesses support 53 percent of the private work force, provide 47 percent of all sales and contribute 50 percent of the gross domestic product. Of the new jobs created in 1994, 62 percent can be attributed to small businesses, a 49 percent jump from 1992. The U.S. Small Business Administration estimates that more than "800,000 new businesses incorporated in 1995, the highest number ever, and a 5 percent increase over the record 742,000 in 1994."

In addition, the Small Business Administration reports that failures and bankruptcies dropped significantly in 1994, and slightly more in 1995. Failures declined from 71,558 in 1994 to 71,194 in 1995. Bankruptcies declined from 50,845 to 50,516 during the same period.

Seeing the Light

Just six months after finding *Secrets of the Pond* in Frankfurt, I flew to Miami Beach for my first American Booksellers Association convention. To me, the event was a delight—beautiful oceanfront promenades, great Cuban restaurants, an evening ride in an open convertible to the Viskaya estate, site of a fabulous party thrown by giant wholesaler Ingram (My goodness, where did all the money come from for this fabulous spread?).

While my accommodations were just fine, many booksellers were disappointed by the funky hotels sold by the local chamber of commerce as "Art Deco Palaces." These were the kind of discoveries Arthur Frommer built his $5-a-day career around in Europe, tiny walkups where the price was right as long as you weren't too fussy. As it turned out, choosing Miami Beach hotels from a convention brochure was a little like taking stock tips from a shoeshine person. As Gainesville, Florida, bookseller Tom Rider explained it: "Many of the rooms were not as carefully restored as the cast concrete and stucco exterior. The lobbies had a lived-in look. He told me that one University Press marketing manager was quite surprised when an elderly resident at his hotel confronted him in house coat and slippers demanding that he change a light bulb.

"He tried to explain his status at the hotel but she insisted, complaining bitterly about the hotel staff."

The marketing man went out, bought a bulb on his own account and returned to the woman's room, finding total darkness. After replacing the bulb, he explained once again that he was doing the job as a favor for a fellow hotel guest, not as a hotel employee. Sure enough, while waiting in the lobby the following morning, the marketing manager was approached by another elderly resident. "I was wondering," the man asked, "if you could change the bulb in my room."

The lights were on when Stuart and Tammy Nixon of Hearthstone Bookshop in Alexandria, Virginia, arrived at their $55-a-night Miami Beach room. Not a bad deal for convention digs. As it turned out, the price negotiated by ABA was just $13 over the maximum legal rate for the room. That's wasn't all. Housekeeping and plumbing problems were obvious at check in. Their double bed was made up with a single-sized mattress pad and single-size sheets. Since the bottom sheet could not be tucked in it quickly became entangled each time they went to bed. The lack of washcloths in the room would not have been a big problem except for the fact that the hotel linen closet was locked up for the night. Cold water was available in abundance. Hot water was another matter. There was none in the sink and the tub water was tepid.

After considerable effort the assistant manager managed to get the hot water working in the tub. When the Nixons asked about the sink, Stuart was astonished by the employee's response: "He said if we have hot water in the tub, why would we want it in the sink. I told him we wanted it in both places and asked to be switched to a room with hot water in the sink. He told me that all the hotel rooms featured cold water sinks. I immediately went to another guest room to test his claim. Within minutes the assistant manager was back with good news. He had managed to draw hot water to the Nixons' sink from the cold tap."

Speaking with a List

These stories, eagerly traded by the convention crowd, provided an entertaining backdrop to the ABA show. I felt like a heretic, thoroughly fascinated by the city's decidedly Latin ambiance, as publishers from larger companies left town early. Darting around the show (I didn't have a booth) it was great fun presenting my first books to potential distributors and, hopefully, salesmen. I remember sitting on the porch of a South Beach cafe, explaining my plan to four Western sales reps. They politely studied the cover of RDR's first woman's book, *Places of Greater Safety.* Every penny I had made from the sale of the press run of *Secrets of the Pond* to Nature Company had gone into this World War II coming of age story. Released slightly before the memoir craze hit in the mid-'90s, this book was a publishing fable, a manuscript that had languished in a drawer for nearly 20 years before it was brought out to great acclaim in England. Now it was coming to America. The reps were unimpressed.

"Where's your catalog?"

"What catalog?" I asked.

"You need a catalog," one of the salesmen explained as a colleague flipped a quarter to a panhandler and took another bite of his croissant.

They had me there. It was obvious I was too small for representation by a sales force. As I began schmoozing with some of the booksellers it began to occur to me that I could sell to stores direct. It's an idea that works and I am certainly not alone.

There is a shift in the balance of power in book publishing. Many stores, unable to compete with deep bestseller discounts offered by warehouse clubs and certain chains, are creating their own bestsellers through staff picks that appeal to customers. Because these lesser-known books aren't being sold at or below cost at competing chains, the independent booksellers can sell them at retail. A case in point is Warren Cassell, a Greenwich, Connecticut, owner of a tiny shop called Just Books.

He and his staff move hundreds, sometimes more than a thousand copies of a literary title that was skipped by buyers at the discount stores and warehouse clubs.

Even some of the largest book chains are pursuing smaller publishers. During the 1994–97 period when our company was getting started, Barnes & Noble's purchases from America's top 10 publishers declined from 74 percent of stock to 46 percent. Most of those sales were picked up by independent and small publishers as well as university presses. This switch, a representative of the nation's leading bookstore chain explained to the *New York Times*, reflected "a wider range of consumer interest in less-known works of serious fiction and nonfiction than has been previously recognized."

But it didn't take long to realize that the Miami Beach reps were correct in one regard, that we needed more titles, at least 50 according to one publishing friend, to make the company viable.

Out of necessity a one-book company started to a longer list. My brother Ron had an idea for a book about female athletes by female sportswriters called *A Kind of Grace*. An original collection of worst travel experiences called *I Should Have Stayed Home* began at a travel writing conference sponsored by Book Passage, a northern California bookstore. But most of that first list came from the same place the company had begun, the Frankfurt Book Fair. I literally tripped over one book, *Dinosaur Gibt Es Nicht*, loosely translated as *There Are No Dinosaurs* by Swiss author Hanna Johansen. Walking through the German Hall, I stumbled on a loose carpet. As I grabbed a table to catch my balance, I looked up and saw the cover image, a chicken-size compsognathus. Obviously this was a rare book, a funny piece of children's fiction about a little dinosaur. Elisabetta Maccari, an Italian born translator who spoke English with a New York accent, agreed to read it overnight. The following morning she offered a plot summary and read sample pages. RDR bought the book overnight and it became our first children's title, *Dinosaur With An Attitude.* Virago, the people who sold us *Places of Greater Safety,* also had three women's travel guides that seemed perfect for the American market. We were also able to line up 20 in-print humor titles from another publisher. By the following spring RDR Books had a list of 29 titles.

New York, New York

As I began attending more shows, it became apparent that arriving early made sense. This was the best way to beat jet lag and, of course, gear up for the show's frantic pace. Many business people believe driving is the easiest way to handle a convention, particularly if you're an exhibitor. John Fremont, a native New Yorker and senior editor with QED Press in Fort Bragg, California, wasn't about to hassle cabs when he went to the same New York ABA convention that dazzled Lewis and Holmes from Hicklebee's.

Fremont knew that you don't just bop into the city after being away for more than a decade. "You take it gradual, starting with New England where they leave their trees unchained," he explained to his wife, a third-generation Californian. "You pick up the pace around Westchester, fine tune your accent and keep your eyes open and your wits sharp as you cross the Bronx, then you hit Manhattan hip."

Fremont's chosen decompression point was Provincetown, Cape Cod's popular resort town where there were few tourists in late May but plenty of "no-parking, tow-away zone" signs.

Letting his guard down, Fremont headed to dinner with his wife after parking his rented Ford Escort in one of the town's many no-parking zones. "The signs mean nothing without a police imprimatur," he told his spouse. "Nobody's going to tow the car!"

Somebody did. The police were less than helpful. "It's a private matter," the desk sergeant told Fremont as he handed over the address of the towing company. "There's been no violation."

"You see," he declared. "I parked legally. I broke no law."

"You want to walk or call a cab?" his wife asked.

The couple walked and got lost until finally stumbling on the yard by accident. Their Ford was the only vehicle in the fenced yard. Fremont was dismantling the fence in an attempt to liberate it when a 19-year-old kid pulled up in a tow truck.

"I been out looking for you," he said, "and you're here causing me grief."

"I want my car."

"You can have it for $100."

"That's outrageous!"

"In New York, it would cost you $150," he said.

"You've stolen my car! You're a thief!"

"Nah, that's my boss. I only work here."

"Well I'm from Manhattan, and I know my rights. I'm not paying!"

"Last week, we had a New York lawyer who refused to pay us, threatened to sue and all?" He said it as a question, as if he still couldn't believe it. "We add $25 a day storage, and it was $200 before he settled, so what kind of lawyer is that?"

It was now close to midnight and Fremont figured he saved $25 by paying right away. The couple drove straight to New York, where sanitation workers were on strike. The city's ingenious inhabitants were dealing with the mounting garbage by tossing it at returning Persian Gulf troops from the city's sky-scrapers. "You've got to love this city," he said to his wife. "Look at those magnificent buildings."

While he was admiring them, his car was taken. He asked his wife if she had seen it happen, but she'd been gazing at sky-scrapers, too. "I told you never to look up when I do. One of us has got to be looking around at all times. Two people look-ing up at the same time makes an inviting target for thieves and pigeons."

"What are you going to do now, Mr. Manhattan?"

"Find a pay phone that works," he said.

"Our thieves are world class, very professional," said the police officer on the other end of the phone. "What do they want with a rented Ford? No phone, no fax. Two to one your car's been towed."

"I wasn't in a tow-away zone," he said.

"All New York is a tow-away zone," the cop told him.

John was soon dodging careening cars near the cleverly concealed pound on 12th Avenue, conveniently located near Javits Center, where the ABA show was in full swing. A tow truck driver hit a puddle as he passed Fremont and drenched him with muddy water, then gave the expatriate a big New York smile, putting to rest the rumor that Manhattanites are unfriendly.

Unfortunately, towing in the Big Apple is not the first-class operation you would expect in a city that knows how to throw a parade and solve a garbage problem simultaneously.

"There were four lines," recalls Fremont. "You waited on the first line to find out if you needed to wait on the second line, which was for people who'd left their registration in their glove compartments. You showed your registration and paid when you got to the front of the third line. You waited on the fourth line for the jitney to deliver you to your car where you could fetch your documents. In the jitney, the driver expounded on how much he should be tipped.

"You don't want to tip too much because then I'm unhappy with what everyone else gives. Too little is worse," he explained, "because it makes me drive erratically when approaching your car. Fifteen percent is perfect, but 10 is OK considering the average tow fee is around $200. What they get you for?"

"Just a hundred," Fremont said, handing the jitney driver a $10 bill, so pleased at being quick witted enough to halve the fine and save $10 that it didn't occur to him until later that he shouldn't have tipped at all.

Back on the street, he confronted further evidence of a decaying economy. "Business stinks," a street person told Fremont as he dirtied the windshield of his ransomed car with a rag for a mere fifty cents. "Reaganomics," the entrepreneurial bum explained, putting a finishing touch on the rearview mirror.

At the airport, Fremont's wallet was lifted. The editor didn't feel a thing.

"These guys are pros," the reporting officer told Fremont. "They can max out a credit card in the time it takes to file a complaint."

Fremont couldn't help but reflect, as his plane lifted off and headed west, that a truly professional pickpocket would've worked the arrival terminal. "How many people leave New York," he asked his wife, "with anything in their pockets?"

The Bodies Beautiful

Fremont's story won an award from RDR Books for the worst ABA convention nightmare. His prize, a night at a bed and breakfast in his hometown, was all part of an *I Should Have Stayed Home* contest sponsored by our company at the Chicago ABA in 1995. When we printed up a couple of thousand *I Should*

Have Stayed Home buttons to promote our book of the same name, it never occurred to me that bus drivers would be trooping through the halls to reach our booth. But they were, along with hundreds of other conventioneers stranded in incredible lines due to hopeless shortages of buses, taxis, Chicago deep-dish pizza, drinks and just about anything else it takes to make a convention go.

The McCormick Center, still under construction, was unable to handle the crush of 40,000 delegates and exhibitors trying to fight their way into a single driveway for the show. Huge lines were everywhere, from registration to the exit lanes. A shortage of table space forced booksellers and publishers from all over the world to sit on the convention hall floor and eat lunch. ABA's executive director Bernie Rath, who had booked Chicago for the next seven conventions, was unflappable. As bus drivers handed out our buttons to customers who had waited up to two hours for a seat back to their hotel room, Rath insisted things would be better in two years, when the new South Convention hall was finished

I Should Have Stayed Home, a book that featured the worst trips of great writers, was followed by a sequel called *I've Been Gone Far Too Long: Field Trip Fiascoes and Expedition Disasters*. When I began working on *After the Death of a Salesman*, many booksellers confessed they had had more than their share of convention nightmares. Diane Leslie had a strange encounter when, as a fairly new employee, a nouveau purveyor of her own passion at Dutton's Brentwood Bookstore in Los Angeles, she was handed tickets to the ABA convention in her hometown. The Southern California show immediately reminded her of the joy she'd "once had browsing Parisian book stalls along the Seine looking for bargains in leather bound literature."

Wearing her most comfortable museum-going shoes, she entered a vast hall, newly built in a shoddy downtown Los Angeles area that seemed far more foreign than Paris. Within seconds her senses were saturated with unearthly sights, sounds and shapes. Diane lost her companions and was left alone to explore the world of booksellers, kindred spirits and kindly bookish souls.

"Where are the books?" she wondered. "There was nothing to do but meander. Outside the convention hall I had seen down-and-outers pushing all their earthly goods in rattletrap shopping carts. Inside I saw only slightly better dressed people carrying, schlepping, wheeling and lugging colossal size shopping bags bulging with posters, balloons and foodstuffs, celebrity aprons, mobiles, calendars and perhaps, I hoped, books.

"I don't know how many miles I was carried in this stream of frenzied humanity but I do remember that, quite abruptly, the pack of us became trapped as if in a dam. Lodged there indefinitely with no room to look but up, I noticed high above us on a platform a ... well ... surely a member of the human race. Was it a man? A woman? I couldn't be certain even though this creature wore almost nothing, just a worried look and a bikini string struck on a body that appeared to be leather stretched over rock. As this unusual performer struck various poses, a most ordinary mortal—was he a publisher?—described the discipline and sacrifice required of female body builders. I admit I was fascinated, or fascinatedly appalled. Then, just when I was wondering what her connection was to the book world, the dam broke and the river rushed me along.

"I drifted aimlessly, not knowing if it was night or day, until a hand grabbed mine, pulling me onto the banks of the Houghton-Mifflin booth. "Come with me," a colleague from Dutton's Brentwood insisted. "We're in line."

"Hours later, when we reached our objective, I found myself standing next to another anomalous creature. Seven or eight feet tall, he had long blonde hair, and his skin glowed with carefully measured sunshine. His shirt was opened to his waist. His ironed jeans were, oh, so tight. A paradisiacal perfume surrounded us, and, my, he could smile."

Even Leslie had heard of the likes of Fabio. "I weel gift yew weeth my book if yew seet on my lap weeth mee," said this not quite Fabio. Then he grabbed Leslie and lifted her high off the ground while a lightning storm of flash bulbs crackled.

"Higher," a photographer urged the giant.

"Get a load of her shoes," someone cried.

Hours later when the not exactly Fabio set Diane back on her feet, he handed her a paperback. She was delighted. "This was the first book I'd seen all day."

"Zees ees from mee tew yew," he said, and then with a smoldering, knowing look he sucked her into his gaze. "Yew must never forget we have pressed zee flesh," he whispered.

Over There

Out-of-body experiences like Diane Leslie's are typical in the nether world of conventions. But nothing produces quite as much adrenaline as an overseas convention. Language barriers, jet lag, exchange rates, customers problems—these are just a few of the many challenges confronted by veterans like Norm Shea, a California specialist in New Age and psychology books. After exhibiting at many conferences in the United States and abroad, Shea knows exactly how to save money on freight. For a Rio de Janeiro convention he sent his samples with a travel publisher who regularly ships to Brazil. At the show he was the victim of one of the worst tragedies that can befall an exhibitor, a booth with no product. The problem with missing trade show shipments is that it is often impossible to trace them in time to do any good.

When Norm realized his books had failed to arrive, he spent all his free time trying to track them down. He even hired a translator to help him work with the Brazilian company. The Californian sat in his hotel room for hours waiting for a call that never came. At the conference, Shea was limited to simply showing off his catalog. By the time the show ended, he concluded that his shipment had been stolen. "I lost $2,000 worth of books."

Good Luck

While losing goods is a problem, location remains, for many traveling business people, the trickiest part of the trade show life. Marianne Sluis of Bookpeople, an Oakland, California, wholesaler, sums up the nadir of the show experience in two words: Las Vegas. She elaborates: "A gaudy plastic hell-hole with the highest concentration of polyester pantsuits in the world." Once she agreed to take on the arrangements for a Las Vegas American Booksellers Association show—making hotel and flight reservations, shipping and setting up the booth, managing the booth staff and keeping a maternal eye on a renegade band of Bookpeople who were including the ABA in their road trip.

"To fully grasp my idiocy in volunteering for this job, it's important to know that I'm absent minded. I take out my keys before boarding a bus, salt my coffee and attempt to read microfiche by placing it in the fax machine. I am, however, a good sport and a soft touch. Bookpeople needed me. I was doomed."

The Bookpeople entourage "stayed in a flamingo-infested hotel on the Strip. It was impossible to walk down a corridor without entering a maze of slot machines through which you could wander, disoriented for hours." The atmosphere was strangely grim. "Has anyone seen a cup full of nickels?" she asked a row of polyester backsides. No response.

Marianne's room faced the Dunes, a club with a minaret-shaped neon sign. This enormous phallic symbol flashed across her window all night.

"Our booth was designed by a Paul Bunyan-style carpenter. He felled a few oak trees, bolted them together and added a few mysterious pieces that keep the booth from toppling over."

As the wholesalers struggled with massive oak beams, other exhibitors pulled out booths made of balsa and styrofoam, snapped them together like Tinker Toys, and were out of there in 15 minutes.

The Bookpeople booth always attracted a lot of attention. Sluis "used to assume that people were admiring its natural grace, but that was before I'd participated in assembling the thing. Now I understood. Our booth was like Stonehenge—people stared, wondering what strange culture created it, how they managed to construct it, and why they bothered.

"After setting up the booth, we realized that the cloth we used to cover miscellaneous boxes was missing. I called around in search of fabric. Las Vegas is not big on natural fibers. We were in danger of having to drape our boxes in feather boas and sequined gold lame'. I finally took an expensive cab ride to a suburban House of Fabrics, where I found something suitably boring.

"As I paid for the fabric, I tried not to stare at other shoppers. They LIVE here, I thought as I got to leave. My mood lifted considerably.

"Searching for decent food in Las Vegas proved to be … well, fruitless. I played slot machines just to stare longingly at the little fruit salad that formed when I pulled the handles.

While nobody developed scurvy during our stay, one reckless member of our staff ate steam tray buffet food and was incapacitated for the remainder of the trip.

"No one will admit responsibility for suggesting dinner at the Alpine Village. It was a dark, almost menacing establishment with stuffed pheasants stapled to the walls, a toy monorail that made spasmodic progress over our heads, and maniacal yodeling music. The waiters wore Naugahyde lederhosen; our waitress wore a plunging peasant blouse that gave her the look of Heidi gone bad. The menu consisted of rabbit dishes that arrived in ominous, gluey sauces.

"Another night we dined in a steak house where, instead of handing out menus the waiter staggered to our table bearing a platter heaped with various cuts of raw meat.

"The show itself wasn't a disaster. Not really. I was trapped for half an hour by the author of a book on surviving hostage situations, but that was appropriate. The underarm of one of my dresses ripped so severely that I had to keep my left arm glued to my side (I am, of course, left-handed). Someone stole the book *Erotic by Nature*, but that happens every year. And one of my favorite customers stopped by the booth, took one look at me, and asked, 'Have you been ill?'

"As we prepared to leave Las Vegas, I looked at my plane ticket. Everyone else was scheduled to leave early that afternoon, but I was booked on a flight that left in the evening. I would never escape this place."

Hysteria was one option, but it was too damned hot for emotional displays. Instead she gave in and hailed a cab. "Take me to the Liberace Museum," she told the driver. "That man was a God."

5

Women on the Road: Against All Oddballs

WHEN I WAS STUDYING at the University of Michigan in the late 1960s, American Motors invited my college newspaper, the *Michigan Daily*, to send one of our editors on a press junket to Florida. I recommended Sue Schnepp, one of our best and brightest, and the publicist freaked. "This is a men's-only event: the wives are staying home," he said with the certainty of one who had been there.

A relic of another time, the male business retreat has long faded into obscurity. In fact, the very idea of men doing business without women present and accounted for is a corporate mistake and a possible invitation to litigation. Except for countries like Japan, where bosses reward good salesmen with prostitutes, the business world knows that women can do as good, often a better job than their male counterparts. It's no secret that many companies now find women better at traveling-sales work than men. From the boardroom to the convention center they are a critical force in the American business community, particularly in the category of new and emerging companies and industries.

Today businesswomen are just as likely to be boarding a red eye flight as men. While the problems they encounter are similar to those experienced by businessmen, there are important differences. Safety is definitely more of a concern for women traveling alone. The simple act of a woman dining by herself is, in some communities, a danger signal, even an invitation to harassment. As a result some women prefer to travel with partners and, at the very least, they decline to take a chance on establishments in secondary neighborhoods. After all, you can never be too careful when you're bringing in the big bucks.

Don't Get the Hiccups

"Once there is a hiccup your trip is over," says Teri Goldsmith, a sales rep who has worked for a number of large companies in the electronics business. Always booked to the max on her sales trips, Teri, who lives in New York, finds that delays trigger a chain reaction, a kind of rolling blackout where it's often impossible to reschedule blown appointments with customers who are themselves overbooked. Diverted by hurricanes, forced to make unscheduled stops when a fellow air passenger has a heart attack, Teri is no stranger to the exigencies of sales trips. Getting a good night's sleep before a New York convention can be a challenge when there's a Judas Priest concert across the street, animal rights activists are picketing your hotel and half naked people are knocking on your door looking for basketball players staying nearby.

Like most experienced international travelers, Goldsmith has discovered language barriers and customs problems can siphon off precious time. It's hard to get a second chance when delays necessitate rescheduling. During her tenure as a sales manager for an electronic equipment distributor, she took a tightly scheduled trip to Europe. She made it all the way to Munich before realizing her French visa had expired three days earlier. Unfortunately it was All Saints' Day and the French embassy was closed. Her flight was scheduled to leave for Paris at 9:30 the following morning. Goldsmith booked a hotel room next to the embassy and spent the night practicing her second grade French and calculating how long it would take to make the trip from the embassy to the airport. Her calculation showed that she would have to obtain her visa by 9:01 A.M. to make the plane. The embassy didn't open until 9 A.M.

Teri was so anxious the next morning she didn't even realize her shoulder pads were sticking out of her jacket as she almost threw herself in front of the first car entering the embassy at 7:30 A.M.

She pleaded with the official to get her a visa.

"That is the worst French I have ever heard," the official replied in English. "And I'm sorry but we can't issue a visa before 9 A.M."

Incredibly, the visa was ready at 9:01 A.M. and she boarded the flight to France two minutes before the doors were locked. Unfortunately her ride was a no-show when she arrived. When she called the office for directions the receptionist laughed and hung up. She tried to call the home office in the United States. The pay phone at the airport would not accept her credit card. Using tokens from the information booth, she finally reached the office. Unfamiliar with the system, she didn't realize that a blinking light on the phone meant put in more tokens or you'll be cut off in five seconds. After three futile calls at a cost of $30, Goldsmith finally connected. The home office sent a fax to her Paris destination and she finally reached her buyer. Unfortunately this woman was no longer purchasing for the company and her replacement was not on board. As a consolation prize the woman took Teri out for a wonderful lunch.

In Denmark, life was easier. Here she let her customer make all the arrangements, including dinner reservations. Joined by his wife, they ate enough for seven people over the course of three hours at a restaurant that reminded her of a cruise ship dining room, complete with ice sculpture. The buyer's wife even ordered multiple deserts. When the check arrived no one made a move. Teri finally paid. The tab looked high but she guessed that with the conversion rate it would only total a hundred dollars. Back at the hotel she figured out the bill was an incredible $700.

The next day the Danes revealed that their company had been recently bought out. But they were certain the new owners would want her products if she would fly back in a few months when the deal was complete. Of course they could discuss the possibilities over dinner. How, she wondered on the way back to Heathrow Airport in London, was she going to explain this to her boss?

At the British security check, her keys set off the metal detector. Officers had a question about the little black container on her keychain. "Oh," said Teri, "that's just a little can of mace my grandmother gave me as a precaution." The Heathrow police arrived quickly, explaining that possession of mace is a federal offense in England.

"I think if you try that mace," said Goldsmith, "it wouldn't work. If I was ever mugged and tried to use it, I would probably spray myself."

With just 15 minutes until flight time, the police searched the American and her carry on luggage. They confiscated both her Swiss Army knife and the mace. She realized that missing the flight would force her to buy a new, more expensive ticket. Combined with the $700 dinner in Copenhagen, she would surely be fired.

As it turned out, Teri was the only passenger to arrive for her flight with a police escort. She made the plane with four minutes to go and did not lose her job.

New product launches are one of Goldsmith's specialties. One of the most promising was an imported watch designed to track ovulation. All a woman had to do was link the timepiece to her monthly cycle. A dial clocked off 24-hour increments, similar to the calendar feature of any watch, helping would be parents track the best time of the month to conceive. Consumers agreed this was a product for our time. Dr. Joyce Brothers was hired to help with promotion.

At the ovulation-tracking watch's trade show debut, the Consumer Electronics Show in Chicago, Teri was sent to O'Hare Airport to pick up Dr. Brothers. Their cab driver's vehicle broke down at the Cabrini Green housing projects near downtown. The two woman, stylishly dressed in suits, walked through the low-income neighborhood attracting stares until they finally found another cab. When they arrived at the show, two protesters were at the booth. One tried to expose the product as a hoax. Another insisted the watch promoted gender exclusion.

Within a month the watch went from a hot product to a baby killer. Even worse, the Food and Drug Administration decided that because the watch charted a bodily function, it had to be classified as a medical product. Importation was banned and the company was instructed to put the watch through a four-year study period.

Getting Along

As Teri Goldsmith knows, doing business in another country can be tricky for women, particularly when men dominate the power structure. Allison Underhill, who lives in Arizona, finds that trying to do business in Asia can be tricky, even though she speaks Mandarin Chinese. Blond and blue eyed, Underhill finds that she gets along much better with men in a foreign environment than women. She thinks that other women are jealous of the way she can get her job done without following all the Chinese rules. "In the Pacific Rim, people won't do business with others until you're friends. Some people don't understand that." In Taiwan she had to work with two Chinese women to implement a computer system. Underhill believed she had all the tools she needed to set up the system on time. What she didn't know was that the entire job would have to be done solo. The women would simply not take direction."I would post notes on the board, talk to them, anything to get them to help. Instead they sat and chatted away, doodled or napped." Later, at a party, a friend revealed her problem. The two big bosses "needed to make an announcement that you were in charge." Allison believes this mistake cost her about 60 days.

Underhill also worked for a company that invested a great deal of money and equipment in a frozen yogurt joint venture. Unfortunately at a ceremony organized to debut the machine, the Americans discovered the hard way that the Chinese did not use 120 volt current. The first machine blew up. It took hot wiring to get the second going.

The Safety Factor

Like Underhill, Susan McConnell, a former sales rep for the Simon and Schuster children's group who now works for Harcourt Brace, understands that every new product is a challenge. And for a woman on the road, safety is a bigger concern than it is for a man.

"I feel that I have to have a third eye about where I am and what I am doing. The number one question when I am traveling is do I feel safe? Safety and convenient access to my accounts are the two most important things I consider when looking for a place to stay on the road. Communication is also a big issue. I need a place where I can plug in my computer and download overnight. The phone system has got to be decent. It's amazing to me how much time I spend on the computer while on the road.

"If I have to eat by myself I go to restaurants where I do not feel vulnerable. One female friend in Los Angeles took a class in self protection for women. For instance, she told me not to park next to a van because women have actually been snatched in L.A."

Behind the Wheel

From Eudora Welty to Arthur Miller, the car has been a central metaphor in the life of the traveling salesperson. In Welty's *The Death of a Traveling Salesman* and Miller's *The Death of a Salesman,* we learn that the highway man tends to be prone to hallucination. He is also a lousy driver. And as Susan McConnell knows, even when you're not at the wheel, simply trying to reach a customer can be a scary experience.

Salt Lake is the kind of place that doesn't always do a very good job clearing its streets. The city was a snowy, icy mess one January morning when Susan and a Simon and Schuster colleague headed to the Brigham Young University Bookstore in Provo, Utah. "Normally this is a 45-minute drive but due to the weather it took us an hour and a half. By the time we reached the campus, the weather was pretty ugly. The road was completely covered with snow and ice. You couldn't even see what lane you were in. My friend began to make a left turn when, to my surprise, I noticed a small Honda coming up on our left. The Honda hit the rear door on the driver's side. Because everyone was driving so slowly, it felt like we were in a bumper car. It would have been far worse on a dry day with everyone driving faster. We got out of our cars badly shaken, exchanged phone numbers and went on our way. Whose fault was it? Under the circumstances, who could tell?"

Later the same day, the two reps went to dinner with two Deseret Book Company Buyers. After their morning adventure, McConnell and her colleague were delighted that one of the buyers would be driving in terrain and conditions more familiar to a local resident. What she didn't know, when she stepped into the car, was that she was on her way to the second half of a Utah driving double header.

"To this day," says McConnell, "we still disagree about whether the jeep made an illegal turn or skidded in front of us. Our driver pumped the brakes and hoped for the best. Again we went into a slow motion skid. The damage was thankfully minimal. Our driver picked up a piece of metal that had fallen off the wheel well rim and offered it to the other driver. She offered to exchange insurance information but the other driver, still in her jeep, wasn't interested. 'I don't see why,' was her response."

When Love Strikes

Another tricky problem for women in business is walking the fine line between work and play. It's a fact that romantic involvements between workers and their supervisors can turn into a quagmire. But in some cases, even the worst nightmare at work can provide a surprise ending. During her tenure as an event coordinator at the Snowmass resort in Aspen, Colorado, Judy Perry went out of her way to hire contractors with special credentials. When it came time to cater a dental convention, she hired a company run by 10 dental students enjoying the good summer life in Colorado.

"I thought it would be perfect for the hotel to hire them for the last night of the show. Not only would they benefit but I was sure the dentists would be excited at the opportunity to meet potential new employees." Then she left town. On her return, Perry's supervisor was waiting outside her office. The barbecue had been a disaster. It had begun raining during the day and the dental students, a little blitzed on beer, failed to think clearly and move everything inside. "I instantly called the dental students, fired them all and explained Snowmass would never do business with them again. I mentioned how unprofessional they were and the potential contacts they had lost.

"The next day I received a phone call from one of the dental students. He made an appointment to come by with flowers, an official apology, and an invitation to dinner. I told him there was no way I would ever rehire him. He said he didn't care about his job and the forgiveness he wanted was completely personal. I agreed to go to dinner and we were married two years later. Not many people can say their boss fired them and then married them."

Fighting Back

Getting tough with men can be a tricky issue for many women in business. Even in first class women discover that their needs can be subordinated to those of male travelers. Fighting back can be an art form. Flying home on United Airlines from a Michigan business meeting, one California executive collapsed into her seat hoping no one would fill the seat beside her:

"Suddenly 15 muscular men fell into the seats all around me. I was convinced that they were returning home after the Tall Men's Association annual meeting in Detroit. Annoyed that I would have to share first class with other passengers, I reclined my seat, ignoring the seven footer's knee sinking into the back of my seat. My conscience took over and I sneaked a look behind me to see if the man was wincing with pain. All

I could see was money and more money. It was everywhere and they were throwing it around carelessly, pushing their seats back laughing and placing thousand dollar bets down on an apparent poker game.

"I leaned back exhausted by the fit exploding from my chest and head, and slipped on my earphones. Just as I began to fall asleep I felt a tap on my shoulder: 'Miss you will have to put your seat back up.' I felt like laughing out loud. I turned to the steward and said: 'You mean to tell me that you are going to make me put my seat back up when every one of these gigantic men is reclining? He looked at me and said, 'Do you know who that is?'

" 'No, and I don't care. But what I do know is that I am not putting my seat back up until everyone else does.' The steward looked mortified but turned to the men and said: 'This lady will not put her seat back up until the rest of you do.'

"Just then Michael Jordan, the only basketball player in the world that I could recognize or identify, because my husband continually talked about his countless commercials, turned from his seat, looked straight at me, smiled and put his seat back up."

Going Solo

Most women who travel in the company of men find there are moments when only another woman can save the day. This was certainly the case for music educator Linda Petersen, who lives in Madison, Wisconsin. Her first ever solo business trip led from San Diego to a convention of music educators in Seattle. In San Francisco the second leg of her United flight was canceled by a Washington blizzard. She switched to Alaska Airlines. But after takeoff the pilot learned the Seattle airport had been shut down a second time. This flight was diverted to the jam packed Portland airport, where her luggage failed to materialize.

After belting down a double Canadian Club Perfect Manhattan, Petersen headed to the ladies room. "I decided it would be a good idea to go to the rest room before boarding a bus for five hours. As I stood up, the zipper to my pants broke. I frantically tried to fix it, but kept hearing our flight number and 'last call' to the bus for Seattle. I closed my trench coat and ran to the departure area grateful the large poster case would cover up my front when I sat down.

"The macho bus driver assured us he would get us to Seattle. I'm from Wisconsin and know you slow down to drive safety in winter weather. This man believed speed was the best approach. We saw countless cars, trucks and vans in the ditches along Interstate 5 and slid across both lanes more times than I care to remember. However, true to his word, we arrived at Seattle-Tacoma Airport — another refuge camp — at about 12:30 A.M. I called the conference hotel, most anxious to get into my warm room.

"The conference hotel told me that due to the inclement weather, they had canceled my guaranteed, confirmed room reservation." She protested, providing her confirmation number, American Express number, yada, yada, yada. The clerk offered her a cot in the women's rest room for $15 per night. She refused it. "I called my significant other in San Diego. He had no words of comfort since I woke him up at 1 A.M."

Only one person was working baggage claim at 1:05 A.M. Since Petersen had switched airlines, he wasn't sure when or if her luggage would arrive. "He asked where I was staying, and I wasn't sure since the conference hotel had canceled my guaranteed, confirmed room reservation. I pleaded for urgency since the zipper to the pants I was wearing had broken. He offered me a safety pin. I refused it."

At that moment a bell captain came by announcing a few rooms were left at the nearby Hyatt. "I ran after him, but by the time I arrived, there were four rooms left for eight people. There was one other woman in the crowd, so we decided to room together. We arrived at the hotel and had all of three hours before we had to get up to work the convention. No one had eaten the entire day, and room service was closed. The hotel vending machines didn't work."

Petersen's new roommate, exhibiting at the same conference, loaned her a skirt and sweater for opening day. "It was at least two sizes too big, and I cursed myself for not accepting the safety pin the guy from baggage claim offered to me."

The exhibit set-up took longer than expected. Linda was unpacking boxes and talking to music teachers while holding her skirt up most of the day. "A fellow exhibitor kept suggesting I wear a micro teal sequined baton twirler outfit from his marching band uniform exhibit. I refused it. That evening all exhibitors were allowed to stay at the conference hotel. I still had no luggage, so the move was quite simple."

After being on her feet all day in someone else's clothes, Petersen was quite happy to settle in for a good night's sleep. However, at 3 A.M. her wing of the hotel was rudely awakened by the fire department. Weather had caused the pipes to freeze and a broken sprinkler line had flooded one of the guest rooms. The entire wing was ordered to vacate. "Fortunately, I had borrowed a football jersey from someone I had just met," says Linda, "so at least I had something clean to wear."

6

Lodging: Rooms with an Attitude

A Sour Note

When Murray Gross, conductor of the West Shore Symphony in Muskegon, Michigan, told friends and colleagues he was flying to guest conduct the San Remo Symphony, many of them imagined him sitting on his sunny Mediterranean terrace sipping Campari in his bathing suit. But as Gross discovered, last night's dream can be today's nightmare.

The guest conductor was smart enough to arrive two days early to get over jet lag Mediterranean style. Gross's problems began when his KLM flight from Amsterdam to Nice was canceled due to a strike by the carrier's pilots. He arrived in Nice the following afternoon and walked over to the deserted train station. There was a transportation strike here, too. No one knew if or when the trains would begin moving again. There were no buses either. Gross spent the entire day trying to figure out how to meet his commitment. Fortunately a hotel desk clerk pointed out that a tour bus was just leaving for Italy. No problem, said the driver who ushered Gross on board with all his belongings. "I'm not exactly going to San Remo," he explained, "but I am going right by it."

The weather was beautiful and the tourists delightful. The

bus zipped out of Nice, through Monte Carlo and on to a fast-moving expressway. The Michigan conductor was just settling in to the trip, his eyes trained on the coast below, when the driver abruptly pulled off into a rest stop. "Here you are," said the driver, as Gross stepped off, thanking everyone profusely. Only after the bus pulled out did Gross realize the driver, determined not to deviate from his schedule, had dropped him off miles from the nearest town.

Walking was out of the question. "I try to pack very light. But when you are a guest conductor you are forced to carry a certain amount of luggage. You have your tails, clothes for rehearsing, all your scores." After failing to find a taxi in his broken Italian, Gross stuck out his thumb. The American hitchhiker asked himself if Leonard Bernstein ever had to do this.

After waiting an hour and a half, he hitched a ride with someone who gave him a lift to the real San Remo exit. Struggling with his luggage, he trudged down the mountain for over an hour, finally arriving at his grand, three-story hotel sweaty and exhausted. The bellhop received a big tip for taking his luggage up a flight of stairs to Gross's room.

Rehearsal began the next morning. "Let's start with Mozart," Gross told the orchestra.

"What Mozart?" replied one of the musicians. "We don't have any Mozart."

This misunderstanding was complicated by the fact that the music for Gross's planned program wasn't immediately available in a smaller city like San Remo. "They couldn't just switch music. To make matters worse the orchestra was extremely talkative and difficult to work with. Eager to show their disdain for conductors in general, the musicians fooled around, wasted time in every conceivable manner, and clearly just didn't want to work." Murray finally "had to really yell at the orchestra, which is not my style."

While this experience wasn't as challenging as a trip to Uruguay, where the musicians walked out because of a political strike and canceled another rehearsal because the building was too cold, it did put a chill on Murray's Italian assignment. After several difficult days, he did score one minor victory. Walking in to the lobby of his hotel after a trying rehearsal, he noticed a sign indicating that the establishment was closed by order of the police. At the front desk Murray learned that an illegal alien had been captured in the kitchen and the authorities were punishing the establishment with a two-day shutdown.

The front desk manager pulled aside Gross, who had five days left on his reservation, and whispered: "We've decided that you can be here but don't tell anyone. If the police ask you anything tell them you aren't staying here."

Within an hour the hotel was entirely vacant except for the conductor from Muskegon. "It was kind of like *The Shining*," says Murray. After resting for a couple of hours, he walked downstairs at 7 P.M., heading to an evening rehearsal. "The door is chained shut from the outside. I can't get out. By now I'm screaming in Italian and trying to climb out a window. Eventually a night watchman who had been out back enjoying the best of the hotel liquor cabinet came and unlocked the door.

"I did three concerts in Italy. Two in San Remo and one in a small mountain town 2½ hours away. My driver was a maniac who swerved around curves at incredible speeds while I was in the back seat getting incredibly sick and wondering if I'd make it."

When he returned to Michigan, Murray told the story in a low key fashion, playing it for laughs rather than pity. "After all," he admits, "it's hard to get any sympathy when you are conducting on the Italian Riviera."

One Room at the Inn

In some cases, rooms are so inadequate that travelers only take them out of necessity. This was the case for singer Kathy Goldmark when she traveled to play a gig at a bar in Hopland, California, and brought along her infant son, Tony, and a babysitter. "I was assured there would be a good place for us to stay and adequate child care. But when we arrived, our accommodations, arranged by a hippie midwife, turned out to be someone's funky camper with no heat. I went into the bar, sang a few songs and then headed out to nurse Tony in the freezing camper. The owner refused to let me bring the baby or the babysitter in the club.

"After the show ended, the band was driven up to a farmhouse on top of a mountain. The other musicians rolled out sleeping bags and I unloaded Tony's Pampers, a stroller and a portable crib. After we were all set up I smelled a gas leak. We ended up driving down the hill to Ukiah where we checked into a motel at 5 A.M. When you're a first time mom you are so nervous. If he had been my fourth kid maybe I would have handled it differently."

Room with a View

Seeing is everything when you travel. And there's nothing quite like a room with a view. One frequent traveler told me of checking in to a room that disappointed him on several counts. The windows faced into an alleyway, which smelled badly. And as he went to put away his bathroom supplies, he opened the medicine cabinet to find that the back had been removed. "I was looking directly into the adjoining room."

Rooms by the Hour

These are the kinds of stories travelers like to tell in the dining car on long train rides. On a trip to Longview, Texas, an African-American woman working with Texas Instruments offered me one of her personal favorites. In the late '50s she and a friend headed off to a college reunion in Memphis. A helpful cab driver had steered her and a classmate to a modest bungalow that would accept blacks back in the days when major chains limited their clientele to whites.

"Everything was fine until morning," she explained, when "we rose and realized that iron bars had dropped down out of the ceiling during the night. We couldn't get out of the hallway. Minutes later the owner arrived and lifted the gates. 'I hope you weren't upset,' she explained, 'I was trying to protect you from our customers.'"

The Stranger

For Ralph Woodward, selling books in the southeastern states for Doubleday and Company in the early 1950s often involved a long day's work and a long drive to the next town. On one autumn afternoon in 1952, booksellers in Birmingham, Alabama, were more eager than usual to stock up on *Peace with God* by Billy Graham and other of Doubleday's latest bestsellers, and Ralph wasn't able to leave the city until late in the evening. The drive to Selma, Alabama, was more than one hundred miles on narrow, ill-paved roads with no moon to light the way. Eventually, he arrived in the small town in the midst of cotton country at 1:30 in the morning. It was not the end of the world, but in those days, in a rough and ready Southern byway, it seemed like it.

Dominating Selma's central square was a huge, old wooden

hotel of the New Orleans gingerbread era ... antique and a bit shabby but still the best accommodation in Selma County. Dead tired, and without a reservation, Woodward approached the registration desk at the end of a vast and shadowed lobby and first noticed the searching gaze of the desk clerk. Something in the clerk's manner made Woodward look up. It struck him as odd that men seemed to be wandering around in the lobby and looking down from the balcony. It was awfully late at night for so many people to be awake in a small town. Not only were they up, but clearly he was obliquely the object of their attention. There was a certain something in the air, a vague sense of hostility, that made him very nervous and sent him immediately to bed with the chain fastened on the door.

At breakfast, the local paper explained the mysterious reception. The day before, a federal agent had been shot down in the woods by the moonshining operators of an illegal still. The welcoming committee of townspeople was awaiting the arrival of an investigator—the federal marshal, the F.B.I.—and had evidently mistaken a mild-mannered book salesman for the fuzz.

"I got out of town (with a few orders), but even more with a definite sense of relief. I think some citizens of Selma did not want their source of corn liquor meddled with!"

Unwanted Visitors

One of the most difficult features of business travel is waking up and realizing that your single room has involuntarily turned into a double. If you're very lucky this entomologist's delight will keep to its side of the bed. If you're not, an early checkout may be advised.

Fortunately, most of these travel companions give themselves away before the lights are out. When *Oakland Tribune* editor Bari Brenner checked into a New York hotel she was greeted by a rat coolly sleeping on the pillow.

I wish I could say these problems are limited to second-rate establishments. But as long as there are sliding doors that open to decks and terraces, bugs attracted by bright lights are going to fly in and make themselves at home. The biggest flying beetle I ever saw greeted me one night on the bathroom wall at the immaculate and very pleasant Hyatt Regency Waikoloa in Hawaii. Tropical Rent-A-Car also has problems with little hitchhikers. At least they did on the last subcompact I rented in Hawaii. These nocturnal cockroaches swarmed about in the back, scurrying for cover as soon as the dome light popped on. Tropical was kind enough to respond with an apology and a day's refund.

Not everyone freaks out over bugs. At the world's largest hotel, the 5,000-room Rossiya in Moscow, I was very upset about the cockroach scurrying across my dresser as I checked in. My friend Alex insisted this was no cause for alarm. "I always tell people to relax and just look upon them as pets."

Since it's impossible for a pet to be anonymous, I decided to call him Gorby. Each night I fell asleep thinking about this little fellow, wondering if we were going to have any close encounters. Fortunately he was civilized, sleeping on the floor and scurrying about the dresser every once in awhile just to be sociable.

In a way, cockroaches are the ideal pets. They don't cost anything to feed and you don't have to keep a lot of litter around for them. My problem was that once Gorby knew the welcome mat was out, it was only a matter of time until his friends showed up. Just thinking about one of them scurrying down the nape of my neck around 3 A.M. was causing insomnia.

There was a moral issue here, too, one that is on the mind of most travelers. When I pay for a room, management is expected to take care of any problems that arise. In this case the natural solution would be to move to a non-infested room. But Alex insisted that was not practical. "It's not just the Rossiya," he insisted. "My friends stay at other major hotels here and have similar difficulties. There's no point in getting upset."

Social Security

Some hotels pride themselves on their security system. But I'm always impressed when I find a place that is so safe security is not an issue. Among them is Monhegan House on Maine's Monhegan Island, an artists' retreat made famous by the Wyeth family and Rockwell Kent, among others. There are no keys here because there are no locks on the door. I was convinced it was perfectly safe until someone stole my lunch.

Not Very Suite

At the deluxe Omni hotel in Los Angeles, I was panhandled in the driveway while waiting for a bellman to take my bags. The bellman never showed. Upstairs, a room clerk said he was oversold and offered me a discounted suite. On the fourth night I was bounced for a company VIP. The new room, half a suite, had one of my light switches in a shared vestibule. In confusion the guest staying in the other half of the suite turned my room lights on at 4:30 A.M. I asked for another room and was told the staff would move my clothes to a new room that afternoon while I was working at the California Gift Show.

When I returned to the Omni at the end of a long day, I learned that the computer had accidentally checked me out of the hotel at 2:30 P.M. After straightening out that problem the front desk had good news and bad news. My new room was made up. The bad news was that the bellmen couldn't find my belongings.

"Has anyone looked in the closet of my old room," I inquired. A bellman was dispatched and sure enough, it turned out that the day staff had forgotten to make good on their promise to move my clothes.

The Dreaded B&B

As many experienced travelers will tell you, it's not necessary to travel all over the world to find bad lodging. Sure I've slept with loud German snorers at a hostel on the Sea of Galilee, flushed out cockroaches from the bathroom at my hotel in Bohol and even been awakened in the middle of the night by a weird guy with a lighter at a virtually deserted campground on the Caribbean Island of Jost Van Dyke. But after sleeping in more than a thousand hotel and inn beds stretching from Shanghai's Peace Hotel to the wilds of Tyonek, Alaska, I can assure you nothing packed more excitement and less glamour than my week at Ellen and Bob's in Manhattan.

As a business person, I've learned over the years that bed and breakfasts are often the best places to stay in big cities. The advantages are obvious. Most B&Bs are owner operated. Instead of dealing with a staff of 18-year-olds, you are in the good hands of an intelligent adult who depends on repeat business to pay the rent, put their kids through school or in the case of my friend Betty, pay for a very expensive opera habit. Betty is an opera addict, and in New York City, where opera tickets can be dear, operating a bed and breakfast is one easy way to pay for orchestra seats. Betty is also my friend, a New Yorker who has hosted me with class on numerous occasions in a wonderful Upper East Side neighborhood. Her apartment has a view and a grand piano, kind door people, fabulous budget restaurants around the corner and a good price —just $80 a night.

Because Betty enjoyed hosting children, I decided that it was the perfect place for my touring author Michael Rosen to stay, accompanied by his teenage daughter Laura. And that was how I found Ellen and Bob. Since there wasn't room for all of us at her place, Betty recommended I stay with them because their apartment was close and safe. Every day I could walk over to pick up my touring author and drive him to appearances in New York, New Jersey or Connecticut.

Check-in at Ellen and Bob's was a breeze. My 1:30 A.M. arrival gave me a chance to meet them in their bed clothes. Bob's pajamas were a bit short in the inseam, exposing part of his calf. Ellen had slipped on a caftan and gave me a big smile through a thin gloss of cold cream. They assured me the apartment was safe as long as I remembered to check the dead-bolt at night and not let in any strangers.

Several years earlier a neighbor had opened her door and was surprised by a lone gunman who put a bullet through her head. The Condo board was still trying to figure out how this creep had managed to elude security. So was the NYPD.

I learned that Bob had some strange ideas about privacy. When I went out to call on stores or assist my touring author, Bob didn't just enter my room. He went through my closet and rearranged my belongings. While I was in the shower he would pound on the door to be sure that the curtain was drawn. And when he learned I had taken a message on call waiting, rather than immediately terminate my phone call, his poor impulse control became obvious.

"You don't understand," he screamed at me in an all too typical rage. "This is a business, that was a potential customer."

"She only called two minutes ago."

"That's not the point," Bob sputtered as he headed off to his bedroom.

Because Bob had gone bankrupt several years ago, he spent a great deal of time focusing on his return to greatness. "You need to know something about me," he explained in one of our periodic chats, "there are two things that I love in the world. One is Ellen, the other is money."

In his heyday, Bob had worked on political campaigns, run multimillion dollar companies and also been an alcoholic. His drinking problem may have contributed to some of his marital disputes. But Bob told me with considerable pride that he had, never, even in his worst stupor, ever hit a woman. Unfortunately he had been victim of domestic violence on more than one occasion. His last marriage ended after his wife broke a wine glass over his head and proceeded to grind the stem into his head. It took 14 stitches to repair the damage.

While Bob professed an almost Gandhi-like belief in the virtues of non-violence, he was not averse to dishing out verbal abuse in the bedroom, the kitchen, the living room or my bathroom. When he found a bit of water on the floor following one of my showers, he rushed in with towels for the floor and a stern warning. His fits of rage were so terrifying that for the first time in my life I began experiencing stomach trouble. It began the moment I entered the apartment and seemed to diminish as soon as I left the following morning after one of his spasms of anger.

Perhaps the single most frightening moment of my stay was the night I woke to Bob and Ellen screaming at one another. They were having another one of their major rows. He was yelling obscenities and she was in tears.

"Are you coming to bed?" she finally asked.

"Never," he screamed as he bedded down on the couch in front of his favorite black and white portable TV.

The following morning Bob was the ideal B&B host, making sure the tea was perfectly brewed, the toast wasn't burned and the banana was peeled and properly sliced for my Wheaties. The sun was lighting up the East River, and limos were lining up for the leaders of the corporate pack on their way to Midtown and Wall Street. Ellen was dressed and headed for work as if nothing had happened the night before. I was glad they hadn't killed each other.

7

Short Subjects

Fear and Loathing in Manila

BUSINESS TRAVELERS ARE often asked to name the most absurd place they've ever visited. In my case that would have to be Manila's Malacanang Palace. I have nothing against rich people, powerful people, even beautiful people. But of the seven deadly sins, none is more peculiar than greed, particularly the variety personified by the most famous size 8 in the history of the Philippines, Imelda Marcos. If it flashed or looked funny, she had to have it. She could not understand the difference between cash and class.

I had come to Manila on business and thought it would be educational to see the liberated Marcos citadel. I knew that Imelda had a shoe fetish but didn't realize that many of her favorites were from abroad. Her husband, former President Ferdinand Marcos, always insisted on domestic footwear. Imelda supported the import market with her feet. What a kick.

What was wrong with these people, I kept asking myself as my palace guide, Mellie Ybanez, escorted me through the halls she and tens of thousands of Manila citizens helped liberate during the People's Revolution of 1986. "She didn't just pick what she liked. She bought everything in her size to make sure no one else could rival her. And the sad thing was only 18 percent of these shoes were made here in the Philippines."

Politics and commerce created a nauseating monument to conspicuous consumption in a country where too many people lack life's basic necessities. "There are over 3,000 pairs of shoes here," Ybanez told me as she led the way through the basement exhibition hall that displays the 25 percent of the wardrobe that the first family was not able to get out of the country by helicopter before the people took the palace. "This is just what we found left behind on the loading dock after they had fled."

Within their own palace wing built at the suggestion of a seer who insisted it would ensure Ferdinand Marcos' re-election, the first family of the Philippines seemed to get by just fine on a civil servant's salary.

With their own barber and beauty shop, hospital, private chapel, Hollywood-style makeup room, chandeliered bedrooms, $7,000 toy cars for the grandchildren and staff of 200 to keep things humming, the Marcoses certainly were the most blessed of the 14 Spanish governors-general, 13 American civil governors and nine Philippine presidents to have lived in this 200-year-old royal house.

Touring the home, visitors gaped at artwork such as the Boticelli-style painting of Imelda Marcos in which she looks like a latter-day Venus coming out of a shell. And not far from the vast supply cabinet with enough medicines to supply a small hospital is an oil of the young swashbuckling Ferdinand making his way out of the jungle.

With their vast bedrooms, libraries, studies and offices, the Marcoses had plenty of room for their extensive collection of fine art and jade. Also here is a small portion of the first lady's jewelry collection.

"She took a lot of the best pieces," explained Ybanez. "But we did find some of the receipts, like the one for six pieces purchased at a New York jewelry store for $1.4 million."

It's hard to know whether to giggle or weep as you walk through the palace halls, making a mental inventory of the millions in tax dollars these leaders spent on helping themselves instead of the people who really needed a hand in this country.

"Of course we donated most of their medicines and some of the medical equipment to hospitals that needed it," said Ybanez. "But we felt it was better to leave some things here so that future generations could better appreciate their history."

Perhaps the leading attraction in Imelda's basement shoe department is her disco shoes with the blinding lights in the translucent heel. "She was something of an insomniac who liked to go dancing in the late hours," explained Ybanez.

Footwear is only one small part of the basement wardrobe room. Looking at the 57 racks of dresses it was obvious she had some unusual ideas. Among the imaginative designs in the outerwear section was a bulletproof London Fog raincoat. "When it fell off the hanger," said the guide, "it was so heavy the guard taking care of this section couldn't pick it up."

Some exhibits, such as the Pampers boxes the first couple used to take cash out of the country, are lost to history, but a hall of fine and decorative arts is showcasing the Marcos school of fashion and design. An entire curated exhibit was created around the shawls of Imelda.

While many things are special about the Malacanang Palace tour, one of my favorites is the private chapel located off the mirrored Hollywood-style dressing room. Four faiths—Hindu, Muslim, Catholic and Russian Orthodox—are represented here.

Like San Simeon, the religious art creates a kind of cathedral to capitalism. Side by side are statuaries of the Three Wise

Men, silver vestments, a picture of the Virgin Mary, Orthodox altar pieces and furniture that Imelda bought in India after attending Indira Gandhi's funeral.

It would be easy to dismiss the Marcos collection as the demented spoils of a 21-year regime. But this denies the possibility that Imelda and Ferdinand had a higher purpose in mind to demonstrate the important role shopping plays in the political process.

On Imelda's nightstand is a mirror with a digital readout of the time across the bottom. When the alarm sounds, the mirror suddenly illuminates with a color photograph of the Marcoses. It is that image, fleeting though it may be, that offers hope to those who have hit the limit on their Visa card.

Going, Going, Gone

Joe Woodman traveled constantly when he worked for a California computer software company. On some occasions he would fly to two cities in the same day. Catching flights could be tough at the end of a long day. Determined not to miss his connection in Portland, he handed his rental car off to a uniformed employee in the airport driveway. What Woodman didn't know was that this employee was thinking about quitting. Receiving the rental car pushed the attendant over the edge. Two weeks later Woodman received a call from the rental company, asking when he intended to return the vehicle. "That's funny," said Woodman. "I thought you got the car back two weeks ago." Eventually the vehicle was found, stripped and abandoned. The employee had fled with the car and never showed up for work again. The hassles that followed went on for months. "I never realized how profitable the rental car business could be," he explained. "The battle went on for months over liability. I finally won."

Bleacher Training

When Mitch Weintraub boarded a New York train enroute to Washington, D.C., for a weeklong sales meeting, he was looking forward to some nice meals. But when he dug into the first of seven boxed lunches, a bite-size sandwich, a mini bag of chips and a tasty radish, he realized no one was going to gain weight on this trip. "The only good thing was that I was able to choose between the Partridge Family lunch box or the one from Lost In Space."

He and his colleagues spent the first two days sitting in bleachers at a high school football stadium somewhere in the District of Columbia. Listening to the marketing executives lecture on company plans he learned that "it is virtually impossible to fall asleep while sitting on bleachers."

After several days in the stadium it was time for R&R. What could be more fun than a bike race? Unfortunately the competition was held in the rain. This could be dangerous, but the company made sure to take precautions. "They made us sign waivers before the race began," says Weintraub. "I guess they did care about us after all. Needless to say, someone did get hurt and had to go to the hospital. Ironically, it was the company's vice president of safety."

Bleacher training went on and on. By the time it was over, everyone was in the advanced stages of fanny fatigue. Fortunately the company agreed to let the sales team fly home. "I was seated next to a very attractive woman who insisted on telling me intimate details of her life," says Weintraub. It turned out the woman was a stripper dating a biker who was 20 years older and looked like Yosemite Sam in leather. She also modeled for a biker magazine.

"While we were taxiing she revealed that she had a kid just

put up for adoption." Weintraub tried to connect by mentioning that he had just adopted a cat from the kennel. Just before the beverages were served, she mentioned she hadn't had sex for twelve days.

On Target

Cheryl Bolen had unexpected delays on the first leg of her trip from Akron, Ohio, to Fort Sill in Lawton, Oklahoma. Scheduled to give classified briefings on successive days at the Army base and the Pentagon, she departed frozen Cleveland for a connection in Dallas. Most of the flight was spent preparing her briefing. In Dallas a thunderstorm put the plane in the number 61 position for landing. After circling for an hour the captain announced the plane was cleared to land in Oklahoma City to refuel. It would have been easy to get a rental car for the hour-long drive to Lawton. Unfortunately the carrier had no gate in Oklahoma. Unable to leave the plane she flew back to Dallas, circled and landed after the last commuter flight to Lawton had departed.

"I checked with the airline I'd come in on. Yes, they would find me a hotel room. Yes, they would pay for a dinner. No, there weren't any vacancies at local hotels; the storm had filled up the hotels earlier in the evening. Yes, they would give me a voucher for dinner at one of the restaurants at the airport. No, there were no restaurants open in the airport and no one knew if any of the restaurants outside the airport were open." Besides it was raining hard. Bolen found an unoccupied bench and decided to spend the next five hours waiting for the first commuter flight to Lawton.

"As I sat there, moving my feet so the cleaning lady could get under my bench, it struck me that I had a briefing document in my briefcase that was classified SECRET. Even though

I didn't advertise that fact, I couldn't chance someone stealing it from me if I accidentally dozed off. They'd be after cash or credit cards, but I'd end up having to report a breach in security, one of those career-shortening events. I walked over to the nearest storage locker. None available. I went to the next one, a little faster now as panic began to overwhelm my tired and tormented mind. There was one left. But someone had stuffed a paper clip into the coin slot. I had to stay awake the rest of the night guarding my SECRET document. That thought was sobering and I began thinking about staying-awake techniques. How about coffee?"

The vending machine, which was out of cups, took her money. After watching coffee flush down the drain twice, she started thinking Coke. The vending machine was stripped of caffeinated drinks. Bolen started walking, several miles in wide circles. She managed to stay awake, memorized the terminal's floor plan and the contents of every display case. She also watched the American flag as it closed down three TV stations.

Shortly after 5 A.M. she took her spot at the commuter airline's check-in counter. She was the first to learn that the flight was canceled. The next flight left at 9 A.M., the time her partner would be briefing the colonel. On the phone she and her colleague agreed they would reconnect in Washington, D.C. His trip to Lawton had been canceled by a family emergency.

After a three-hour delay, Bolen took off for the East Coast. A blizzard in Washington had snarled National Airport, where a plane had slid off the runway into the Potomac. While there were no injuries, the accident forced other flights, including Bolen's, to circle for two hours. She arrived at her Crystal City hotel at 1 a.m and learned that her guaranteed-late-arrival room had been sold out from under her. Another room was available in a downtown hotel.

The location, next to the Greyhound Bus Terminal, was central. "My room was on the third floor, directly over the parking lot for the buses. The smell of diesel fuel filled the room, but it was the droning rattle of the diesel engines that made it hard to sleep. That and the swayback bed with a full 12-inch valley at its center. And, of course, the knocking steam radiators under the frosted windows were never in sync with the engines."

On less than two hours sleep, Bolen made the presentation that was instrumental in winning approval for a major missile program.

Tale of the Tape

Airport traffic cops know that businesspeople always wait until the last minute. No matter what time the flight takes off, they always cut it too close, dashing across driveways, risking accidents to make their flights. And inevitably, they also push their luck in the luggage department. Oakland, California, airport officer Lashanda Richards tells this story: "Man walks out of the terminal with a duct-taped suitcase, starts walking across the traffic lane and sure enough, the suitcase bursts open, spilling clothes all over the driveway. He pulls all his stuff together, jams the suitcase together and then starts rewrapping the duct tape around the case. Of course the case won't close so he's half sitting on it as he tries to rewrap. Finally, he gets enough tape around it to partially close the case. The guy picks it up and heads off to the parking lot with clothes dangling out the bottom of the suitcase, brushing the ground."

Undress for Success

Sex in strange places is a tricky and risky business. Of course, the traveling salesman has a long history as a sexual predator.

Some groups such as the Gideons were founded on the premise that they needed to clean up the horrible image of the traveler. What, after all, was the traveler but a big-city satyr eager to corrupt innocents in small towns across the land?

Traveling salesmen jokes passed down through the generations can even be found on the Internet. But it's worth noting that in some cultures the old ways die hard. In Japan, salesmen who do a particularly good job are rewarded with all-expense-paid trips to South Korea. Wives dutifully pack their condoms and these top dogs are off for a memorable Undressed For Success tour.

According to Eunice Kim, executive secretary of the Asian Church Woman's Conference, the brothels of the Pacific Rim remain one of the business world's greatest hazards. From Taipei's Peitou to the streets of Manila, she is intimately familiar with the nightmare of sex tourism. The leader of an international campaign to stop the exploitation of impoverished Asian woman by affluent travelers, Kim has documented this issue in three books. "Whenever I travel," said Kim, "the first place I visit is the Red Light district."

This problem is most obvious in places like Thailand's Pattaya, a beach resort two hours from Bangkok where European businessmen travel by charter jet. On arrival they are taken to bars or clubs and set up with women for the week. Walk along the seashore here and you'll find palm after palm sheltering a sugar daddy with his young pay-for-play date. With the notable exception of China, where an apprehended prostitute and a john will wind up in the pokey, most Asian countries have not been able to abate this epidemic. In South Korea, says Kim, tourist associations have actually run courses for aspiring Kisaeng (prostitutes).

In some cities this instruction is required of any Kisaeng

who wants the ID card necessary to pass through hotel gates. This curriculum one-ups the old prostitute-with-a-heart-of-gold role that has been played by actresses ranging from Shirley MacLaine to Melina Mercouri. Here women are told that selling their flesh helps the GNP by bringing in badly needed foreign exchange.

Much of this money comes from Japanese businessmen. In exit interviews 80 percent of them agree that the most impressive thing about Korea is Kisaeng parties. Some were so enthusiastic that they promoted Korean prostitutes to field wives and reserved these women for themselves and a few close friends. Working with her fellow churchwomen, Kim has documented sex tourism across Asia. Virtually enslaved to brothel owners, perpetually in debt to pimps who heavily garnish their paychecks, exposed to all manner of sexually transmitted diseases and frequently victimized by their johns, these aren't very happy prostitutes.

But the noble church campaign to stamp out these abuses is frequently met with contempt and derision by those who could put a stop to it. "The hotel owners think I'm crazy," Kim told me over tea and cake in the lobby of a major Seoul resort hotel. "The governments look the other way. When I talk about the risk of AIDS, no one seems to care."

With guidebooks promoting Korea as "a paradise for men where Kisaeng girls can be picked up like a slave girl in the slave market," it's understandable that there is considerable demand for these services. Some participants in the church conferences hosted by Kim's group have learned about the problem first-hand.

"After one meeting a New York minister went back to his hotel room" she explains, "and got an urgent call from a woman who identified herself as Ms. Kim. He thought I was calling about an emergency and said come right over. But when he answered the knock on the door a few minutes later, it turned out to be a Kisaeng using the Kim name as a pseudonym. She was furious when he sent her off and kept calling every hour demanding to know: 'Why do you turn me way?'"

Unable to change a country that gives the green light to the red light district, Kim has gone to Japan to confront the sex tourism industry face to face. "I've lectured Japanese women's groups, telling them they should insist on traveling with their husbands to Korea. They reply that the problem is hopeless. 'They won't let us come,' one lady replied. 'Besides, he feels it's his right to go. He loves young girls very much and I can't do anything about it.'

"This kind of talk is very frustrating," she told me. "We need to teach these men that the best way they can show their love for these young girls is to leave them alone."

8

The Back Office: Is Anybody There?

No MATTER HOW GOOD a job you do in business, it's comforting to know that your future often depends on people you'll never meet. Poised at the other end of an 800 line, frequently in another time zone, they typically introduce themselves by their first name and have a peculiar fascination with the last four digits of your Social Security number. With a single keystroke they can decide when your check is cut (and actually mailed), your order is shipped and whether to take your first-born son.

The old community model, where people did business with folks they actually knew, is a dim memory. Seldom, if ever, do we get a chance to meet the people who create the goods that shape our lives. Instead of creating businesses around communities where anyone can earn enough to own a house and support a family, production is outsourced to Third World countries where minimum wage is computed in cents not dollars. Banking is done offshore, frequently in a country where no one steps outside with anything less than #15 sunscreen. Customers are known by their international freight forwarders and payments are made by letters of credit or wire transfers.

When the existentialists were talking about alienation they

never realized that they were perfectly describing the cocoon of the global business person in touch 24 hours a day via cellphone or the Internet but never quite sure what to say. Especially when you get recordings like "the person you are trying to reach has left the cellular calling area. Please try your call again later." Whenever I do pierce the veil of voice mail the shock is so great I'm speechless. And all too often the news is disappointing. After all what can you say when you discover, as I did in the middle of publishing my first book, that the printer handling the job was broke and couldn't afford to buy paper? What can you do when you get a bill from United Parcel Service for Saturday pickup at a company that is closed on Saturday? How can you respond to a wholesaler who deducts money off your check for the return of a product you never sold them in the first place?

You can say the same thing millions of intelligent business people say every day of their lives, "The inmates are running the penitentiary." Actually that's not quite true. In the case of airlines like TWA, the inmates are often taking your reservation calls at a prison in Ventura, California. To me the very thought of giving my credit card number to a convicted embezzler demonstrates that big companies really do have a sense of humor. Do you really think that a convicted check forger is going to be inclined to volunteer information on an unpublicized half-price bereavement fare to your grandmother's funeral? Fortunately the airlines haven't outsourced any engine repair work to prison industries—yet.

Even if they don't have a criminal record, there are times when you wouldn't mind putting a few of these back office people in a holding cell for a couple of hours. The most carefully constructed deal can founder on a freight shipment that goes astray, a bank deposit that is misapplied or a canceled flight. And yet, were it not for the people in the back office who crunch the numbers, move the goods and fix the broken computers, it's doubtful that the modern business person would be able to get through the day. No matter how good a job the salesperson does in the field, the success or failure of a deal often depends on a company's ability to fathom the complex rule book of large customers. And in some instances the rule book governing matters like freight shipments can hit 60 pages.

In certain cases it is necessary to temporarily suspend or even terminate business with a major account. Because they deal in large volumes with thousands of customers, these companies have a difficult time handling the special needs of their suppliers, such as getting paid. Because small businesses often must sell on terms that are less favorable than large customers, their margins are very short. Problems such as late or non-payment, accounting discrepancies, return of goods in unsaleable condition or preemptive changes in the way bills are paid can turn into a life or death matter.

Perhaps the most difficult problem of all for many businesses is finding a reliable supplier, one that is free from defects in workmanship, labor unrest, dock strikes and staying above the waterline in floods. My very first book sale, 5,000 copies of *Secrets of the Pond*, was blessed, or so I thought. For one thing, more than 100,000 copies of this title had been previously sold to customers in other countries. At the Frankfurt Book Fair I held an excellent sample of the product in my hand. My order for the American edition was good and the printer in China was guaranteed payment through a letter of credit. All he had to do was get the books to California in acceptable condition and the bank would release his payment.

To make sure everything was going right with the job I

hired a Hong Kong printer, Philip Choi, and sent him to the Chinese company's plant for a prearranged inspection of the first 500 sample copies. On arrival he discovered a problem that threatened timely delivery of the product to Nature Company. There were no books. I guessed that the printer was short on cash and unable to afford the paper he needed to run the job.

"We were very concerned to learn that you did not send the four samples of *Secrets of the Pond* as promised last week," I wrote him. "In addition Mr. Philip Choi informs me that you did not ship 500 copies of the book on May 27, as required by the letter of credit.

"Since he did not see any printed copies of the book on his visit to the plant it appears that this title has not gone to press. I am wondering if you have had difficulty obtaining paper for this job due to a credit problem with your paper supplier. I might be in a position to work something out with you.

"Perhaps there is another problem. Please do not be embarrassed to tell me what your problem is."

Sure enough the printer replied that "we did have some credit problem with our paper supplier in the last month."

A couple of weeks later the first 500 books arrived via air freight in good condition. Meanwhile, the bulk shipment of 4,500 books left by sea aboard the OCCL Freedom. Barring a typhoon, everything was set.

But while the ship was on the high seas, the packager of the books in Europe decided to cancel his guarantee of payment, the letter of credit. He was now insisting that I pay for the books on arrival. This meant I no longer had the right to inspect and approve the goods before handing over the money, as arranged by the letter of credit. Of course the seller was taking a chance. He knew I had the right to refuse the books and send them back to Hong Kong on the next boat. But he guessed, correctly, that I was not about to abandon my customer. You can imagine what it felt like, after putting down a cashier's check for $20,000, to walk into a South San Francisco warehouse and begin spot checking boxes one by one. The books were good, thanks in part to Philip Choi's careful advance inspection at the Chinese plant. The deal went through with Nature Company and RDR Books was born.

In some instances, when the back office is particularly hard to deal with, it does make sense to just say no. Many businesses use this approach when they are dealing with a customer that has a long and complicated history. Here, for example, is how our company handled one of these situations with a large wholesale account. This letter, written by RDR Books' office manager, was sent more than five months after we suspended shipment of books due to a series of business difficulties.

First of all, let me thank you for the many orders that your company has continued to send us even while we were both trying to clear away the financial issues that were in the way of our moving ahead with our primary business of selling books. There are only a few more outstanding invoices to settle (See attached statement.), and then we'll be able to ship you the thousand or so books that you have on order with us. Your company is one of our best customers, and I'm sure that you'd like things to start moving again as much as we would. I've spoken to many bookstore owners that buy from you, and they all express concern that our books are temporarily unavailable to them from you.

As I said, your company has been a great RDR Books customer in many ways, but there are a few problems that I'd like to bring to your attention, and then go on to make a few suggestions on how we'd like to try to avoid them.

As you know, we are a small, steadily growing publishing house whose major strength is in developing books that are fun, well written, sturdily constructed, attractively designed, and, above all, have a long-lasting appeal. All of our books have become standards, with ever-growing appeal. But though our books are excellent sellers, the point that I want to emphasize here is that we are a small company. We have a very effective staff, but naturally, given our size, we are limited in the amount of time that we can devote to serving individual accounts. Please consider this list of some of the problems that we have consistently had with your company. As you will see, they have to do with two major areas: Your company's return/chargeback practices and its payment policies.

1. Your company's returns and chargebacks regularly create costly time-consuming problems for us. Here are some of them:

a. Warehouse returns are *always* a disaster. We are almost obsessive about packing our books so that they arrive at our customers in pristine condition. We bubble wrap them tightly in small bundles and ship them only in new boxes. However, every return that we have ever gotten from your warehouse has been packed with extreme carelessness, with no padding of any sort. The books are simply tossed into a recycled box and sent out to us in a condition that makes them impossible to resell.

b. The information on these forms is very inadequate. Phone numbers change without notice; deadlines are imposed (for damaged returns) without being indicated on the form; not all return issues are covered on the form; it is not clear who to contact for some problems; and when we try to contact the Returns Department by phone, we only get to leave messages on an answering machine, never receiving a return phone call. We recently spent 3 days, faxing some 30 or 40 times to the fax number indicated on an up-to-date Refused Return form, only to learn later that that fax number was no longer operable.

c. We have several times gotten notices from your Accounts Payable departmant saying that shipments had not been received, when they had in fact been received. Once we have gone through all of the time-consuming research in our records, and requested Proof of Deliveries from our shipper to prove that the order was indeed received by your company, and then processed the form, passing it on to your company, it then takes about three additional months for us to get payment.

d. Your company deducts return chargebacks from our checks before giving us a chance to respond to those chargeback claims. There are often problems with your returns, so we are obliged to fill out your Refused Returns form in meticulous, time-consuming detail. It can then take as much as three months to get monies that are legitimately owed to us. Recently, we got a 50% "settlement" of unacceptable returns that should have been paid back at 100% a year and a half ago. In short, we were penalized because of your company's failure to respond to us in a timely manner.

e. We recently received the return of a book that was not one of our publications. We had spoken to officers in your company about this return a month before the return item actually reached us. We then placed several phone calls and sent several faxes to find out who at your company handles this sort of problem. We finally got return information, filled out the form, and received notice from your Returns Department that they were denying the claim. We then had to call your company to inquire about it, and a couple of months later, we received an adjustment of this credit that should never have been taken in the first place.

f. We had filed a timely response to a chargeback claim that your company had taken on a fairly large number of books that had never in fact been returned to us. It was never clear who precisely the claim should have been sent to at your company and nobody bothered to inform us. We were so used to waiting long periods for responses from your Returns Department that our staff, having other things to do, put our paperwork aside until we heard from you. We never heard and simply forgot about the claim. We recently made the time to reassert the perfectly straightforward claim that the books had never been returned to us. We had all the paperwork, and even saved the box that the return was supposed to have come in. We contacted the shipping company to find out the weight of the box as shipped to determine the possibility of that box being capable of containing the alleged return. We contacted Accounts Payable, informed them of the impossibility of the particular shipment containing the number of books claimed, we sent in the paperwork indicating the shortage claim. Accounts Payable agreed that they had never sent those books back to us, but then only allowed us a 50% "settlement," making us sign an agreement, as part of the "settlement" that we would never again file a claim for unaccepted claims from 1996.

g. For *every* chargeback invoice that your company has sent us for more than ten books, it has *always* charged us back more than you have actually paid for the books returned. I say this without exaggeration. (I enclose a recent sample of one of your chargebacks, with two credit invoices: one indicating the proper chargeback and one indicating the chargeback that you took.) The overages are about 15 to 30 cents per chargeback invoice. We do not file for adjustment, because the time involved in doing so is prohibitive. We simply take the the time to adjust our amount *line by line* to make them in accord with your line amount. Our Accounts Receivable department estimates that we lose about $50.00 per year with these upward adjustments of the credits that we give you.

h. You have recently initiated (without any prior warning) the policy of not only immediately deducting chargeback amounts from your checks before giving us time to respond, but also deducting amounts from hypothetical chargebacks that you might make in the future. Aside from the cash flow issue that this creates, it makes processing your payments very complicated.

2. Your payment schedule also presents us with complications. As I said, we are a small company, and any delay in payments presents us with problems in every other area of our endeavors. It stalls projects, limits our ability to develop in other ways, and if an expected payment does not arrive, it plays havoc with our everyday operations.

a. Our agreed upon payment terms are 90 days from the date of the invoice, but the invoices are not paid in accordance with this agreement. The payments usually come after 120+ days.

b. As I noted above, you unilaterally decide the legitimacy of a credit, without giving us time to respond before the credit amount is deducted from our check.

c. You recently established, *without giving us any indication beforehand,* the policy of withholding a large percentage of what we expected in payment, thereby forcing us to short circuit some of our current projects in order to correct for the sudden loss of expected income.

... I want to emphasize that in many ways I have been very pleased with RDR Books' relationship with your company. I am eager for us to move ahead and get back to business in a way that will be fruitful and fair to both of us. I'm sure you agree that that is the only way for us to prosper together.

This Heinzian variety of back office problems is just one example of the way commerce can be interrupted. And it points up one of the reasons why high technology has not solved some of the fundamental problems that reach back to that old marketing question posed by my friend Valerie Ryan at Oregon's Cannon Beach Book Company, "How do you get two tons of chickens in a one ton truck? You keep 'em flying."

In many instances the heart of any enterprise, making a quality product at a fair price that people really need, is short circuited by the very technology designed to improve efficiency. As just demonstrated in that letter to the wholesaler, the rule book is often so complex that it's difficult, at times impossible, for companies with a common interest to work together. Emerging companies are often given less favorable discounts and terms than their larger competitors. Often they do not have squadrons of clerks to tend to the picayune requirements of giant companies.

The real loser in this process is not small companies or even the public at large. Rather it is the large companies who deny themselves important new business. They themselves become less efficient and ultimately unable to keep pace with the business at hand. When you read stories about downsizing it's usually because the company lost contact with its customers and vendors.

In my business, getting ahold of people on the phone with new product information, arranging appointments or a simple conversation is the wellspring of business creativity. Few great deals take place in a vacuum. They are usually the result of a creative partnership between a buyer and a seller. The number one obstacle is often the very technology peddled to make business more efficient. I fear that future historians may write that the decline and fall of America began the day voice mail gained half the national market.

Buying a voice mail system is a little like hiring an armed felon to rob your house. Voice mail makes all the mistakes people normally get fired for: wasting time and losing money, losing business, and, worst of all, sleeping on the job. When the whole system crashes much of the community collapses into telecommunications gridlock.

When I called the Grand Canyon with a guidebook research question for the ranger, the machine age had clearly taken over. "This is the Grand Canyon National Park," began the voice mail. "If this is an emergency please say, 'This is an emergency.' If this is not an emergency, please remain silent."

I remained silent. A few seconds later the voice said, "You have signaled an emergency. We are dialing 911." I heard a click, then a dial tone. The system had hung up on me.

I particularly hate voice mail systems that hang up on you when you fail to unblock caller I.D. I'd be happy to identify myself if they would simply answer their phone. If these people don't want to take my calls, why don't they simply go back to smoke signals. Another problem for sales people is the introductory message that goes on for minutes before they tell you how to reach someone who can actually handle your questions. I was totally humiliated by a call to a buyer at San Francisco's DeYoung Museum. His dead letter version of voice mail did not take messages. The only way to reach him was to write a letter. I did so two years ago and am still waiting for an answer. This is hard on someone who has never adjusted to a world where people are so busy talking on the phone they don't have time to see you any more. If our civilization is on the cutting edge, I'd like to know why I'm always getting cut off.

This "Don't Call Us, We Won't Call You" school of phone etiquette has, in many instances, dismantled the entire concept of "scientific salesmanship." A talented sales rep shared my frustration at a Harbor Springs, Michigan, trade show organized by the Mole Hole group of gift shops: "I'll get in my car and drive 500 miles to avoid making a phone call."

Some customers are so hard to reach that potential sellers realize that the only way to make a deal is to adjust to their buyers' circadian rhythm. Teri Goldsmith, a sales rep from New York mentioned in Chapter 5, found it was impossible to connect with a key customer at Sears. After weeks of trying to pin him down for a meeting on one of her lines she asked, "Isn't there a time when you aren't busy?"

She wound up with a 4:30 A.M. appointment at the Sears Tower. The good news was that street parking right outside the front door was free. The entire 102 story building was dark, except for his office. After their session, she checked around and discovered that the buyer, a true insomniac, started his day at 3:30 A.M.

As Goldsmith has discovered again and again, it is often quicker to hop in a car, board a train or plane and go to see a customer than it is to reach them by phone. Often the results are considerably better. Part of this is a credibility issue. Who among us would ever consider giving a roofing job to a contractor they never met? In retail it's much easier to deal with a seller face to face when you can see the goods and discuss how to market them. These meetings are often a good way to prevent back office problems and actually get to know the behind the scenes people who can make everything work smoothly.

But if technology, in the form of the automobile, the airplane and the computer, has shortened the lead time between home office and the buyer's inner sanctum, it has also created a new kind of conflict, one that broadens the gap between the traveler and the customer.

Consider the computer. Book sales rep Susan McConnell, also from Chapter 5, faithfully downloads her sales reports every day when she's on the road. Unfortunately, she reports, "in many instances, it has taken the rep and the buyer further away from the book." In back offices across the land, crashes, upgrade difficulties and a myriad of other problems actually make some reps wish for the return of the abacus. At its worst, problems with an upgrade, such as the one Seattle-based book wholesaler Pacific Pipeline installed, have made it virtually impossible for a company to do business at Christmas time. In Pipeline's case this hitch led to a tragic bankruptcy in 1997 that put many people out of work and hurt suppliers across the country. And back office computer problems also lead to bureaucratic problems on the sales floor.

"Those of us who grew up reading, going to libraries and

buying books have a general idea how the store is set up and how to find things," says McConnell. "We read the trade press and reviews and at least have a sense of what a book is about. There is a new generation of bookseller coming up who is much more comfortable with the computer. This new bookseller is not necessarily a reader or perhaps they only read certain things like science fiction or mysteries.

"There are accounts who really know how to use their computer and others that try to compare apples and oranges to arrive at an order quantity or just depend on their memory. Buyers who are really on top of it order on a regular cycle and take advantage of publisher backlist specials.

"Stores out of touch with their inventory don't know what is selling and are not ordering on a regular cycle. I have seen instances of new and basic backlist arriving in May and being returned in June. Other stores are overinventoried with books they don't need and can't sell and not bringing in the titles that turn.

"I don't claim to know my accounts better than they do. I trust them to know what works in their stores and what doesn't. But as a publisher's representative, I know my list. I have a button that says 'Trust me, I'm a professional.' Sometimes I feel reps are an under-utilized resource.

"Computers have certainly changed the ways we do business. In some ways it's an improvement and in others a step backwards. I don't miss doing physical inventories, but computers distance us from the inventory. The buyer at one large independent bookstore shared a story with me about training a new employee. She told the young salesperson that, in the time it took her to look up the title on the computer, she could walk to the shelf, find the book and the customer would be in line to pay for it."

Another common back office problem is relying on someone 2,500 miles away. Even with the computer, phone, fax, e-mail, express delivery, United Parcel Service and the post office, logistics are the bane of many business travelers. They've learned from experience that handing all the details off to someone else can be a mistake. Ira Steingroot, a well organized and experienced bookseller at Cody's in Berkeley, California, discovered what can go wrong when his publisher, HarperCollins, subcontracted with a publicist to promote his new Hagadah, used by Jewish families and congregations at Passover celebrations.

After a brief stop in Chicago, Steingroot flew off to make three appearances in the Washington, D.C., area. To keep expenses down he was booked at a rabbi's Virginia home. "They gave me a bagel and cream cheese when I arrived. By the time I left I was starving." The food was better in Rhode Island, where Steingroot was scheduled at a Providence synagogue. He headed off to the synagogue to greet an impressive crowd of 60 people at an incredible feast. Due to a miscommunication, a prearranged order for 50 books never arrived. The audience would have walked out empty handed were it not for the fact that Steingroot managed, at the last minute, to scrounge up 10 full price copies at three local bookstores.

These and other back office foulups persuaded Steingroot to abandon his publicist on the Toledo leg of his tour where he sold 140 copies of the book thanks in part to advance coverage in the *Detroit Jewish News, Toledo Jewish News* and the *Toledo Blade.* "My mother and sister went all out to cater the event and it was beautifully organized and arranged," he wrote his publisher at the trip's end. "You would have done well to have hired them rather than the publicist for the whole tour."

9

On the Town: Don't Drink to This

You Say Potato, I Say Ptomaine

WHEN CALIFORNIA PUBLISHER Cynthia Frank signed up for a Chicago convention her partner and husband told her she'd best book a single and go without him. "I was in Chicago in 1968," he apologized, "and they arrested me. My stomach still heaves when I think of the food they served in jail."

Thanks to her first-rate staff, there would be no problem managing the booth without him. The first night she invited editor Sal Glynn, salesman and chef/caterer Mark Wallace and publicist Teresa Simon to dinner at a Thai restaurant. After a long afternoon setting up their booth at the McCormick Place they were hot, hungry and ready to play. Dinner first, followed by a show at Buddy Guy's Legends.

Frank slept soundly that night in her Essex Inn room, not realizing that her colleagues were putting the Michigan Avenue establishment's plumbing to a serious test.

"Ptomaine is not fun," says Frank. "First you're afraid you're gonna die; then you're afraid you're not gonna die. Sal and Mark were hit so hard by the nasty bug they hallucinated as they crawled to and from the facilities." Although their needs were violent and immediate, they were able to take turns, "passing one another on hands and knees like foundering ships on a coal black night."

At dawn Frank could tell from the sounds next door that Simon wasn't doing well either. Then the publisher noticed a whimpering sound at the door. It was Wallace outside, lying on the carpet.

"I can't walk," he told her, "We'll try to meet you at the McCormick Center in a few hours if we're not dead." Without another word he turned around and crawled away.

At the convention hall, Frank finished setting up. Wallace came lurching down the aisle looking rather green.

"Thought you could use some help. Gotta chair? Omigod, where's the head?" Simon was ill, he reported and Glynn, overcome with dehydration, had drunk his way through the in-room refrigerator and was now besieging room service.

"Would you pick up some Gatorade on your way back to the hotel?

Frank ran to a meeting and returned to the booth for an author reading. Wallace returned to his room, replaced by Glynn, who propped himself up in a corner of the booth looking like a cardboard celebrity cutout. He emitted brief sentences, punctuated by low moans.

"I'm afraid to sit down."

"Somebody stole the damn T-shirts."

"Teresa is desiccated, gesticulated, defecated."

"I'm going back to the hotel."

"Don't forget the Gatorade."

When the show closed, Frank headed across downtown looking for a grocery. She found one on a side street populated by blowing trash, winos and mangy dogs. It was a store out of her childhood. A slow fan in the ceiling stirred slower flies. A wood floor, dust on all the jars and can tops. She found a flavor of Gatorade that was no longer made and purchased three large bottles.

On her way out the clerk said: "Welcome back, honey! We haven't seen you here in a while."

At the hotel, the crew was recovering. Everyone was convinced the culprit was the peanut sauce in the blue bowl. Frank said a prayer of thanks to her special lemongrass angel who placed the red bowl closer to her hand.

Wallace, ever the caterer, suggested a visit to the Thai restaurant was in order: "We don't want anyone else to go through this, right? We'll be discreet. We'll tell them to throw out the peanut sauce and start over. If they insist, we'll have a pot of tea with the manager and theorize why the reclining Buddha is so supine."

The restaurant manager was skeptical. "Sick? You don't look sick." Glynn offered to throw up on his shoes. The manager said, "You don't fool me with this trick."

Wallace explained that they weren't trying to sue. "Sue?" the manager heard. "You dare to accuse my cook of making you rich."

When the owner showed up, Frank was amazed: "He frothed and shook like a fine Bearnaise, accused us of being worse than Cambodians and then searched for something worse, finally, with great satisfaction calling us 'book reviewers.'" Soon the group was chatting with the restaurant's attorney in a quiet corner of the restaurant. After a long conversation the attorney told the manager to give the Californians a credit on their dinner.

The manager was delighted: "We fix you dinner to die for."

Friend of the Library

During his tenure as marketing director for a major New York publishing house, one of my friends discovered that sex shows were popular with conventioneers. At the Frankfurt Book Fair he accompanied a group to the Krazy Sexy Club. Each performer walked out onto stage fully dressed. Suddenly all their clothes were yanked off by invisible wires. When the show ended each of the performers, fully dressed again, walked out to mix with the audience. "They ordered a round of apple cider for the entire table. After several drinks, the bill showed up. It was $535."

Since the convention was a marketing expense, the marketing director paid the bill. He was given a receipt that read "$535 contribution to the Frankfurt Public Library."

Blood Brothers

In May 1997, Hank Kaestner, head of spice procurement for McCormick and Company featured in chapter 2, visited the vanilla plantations south of Kunming in China's Yunnan Province. At the end of his trip his hosts held a banquet for the American at the Drunken Fish restaurant, famous for a special dish made from fish that swim in alcohol until they die. Because he had been honored in similar fashion on previous trips, Kaestner knew the drill. In Beijing he had been offered the head of a duck. In Shanghai he had been served the head of a fried chicken. And in Indonesia he was served the delectable head of a fruit bat.

Entering the restaurant Kaestner saw a large wicker style basket containing large, live snakes. Since he preferred snake meat to fish heads, he asked his host if snake could be added to the menu. No problem.

In the private dining room wonderful appetizers spread across the table include the month's specialty, fried bamboo caterpillars. Fifteen minutes later a waiter arrived with a fruit juice sized glass containing a red liquid.

"What's that?" Kaestner asked.

"Oh, that's the blood of the snake that you picked for our dinner," responded his host."

"Why did the the waiter bring it to our table," he asked.

"You and I are going to toast with it."

The blood was poured into shot glasses. Kaestner thought about asking if he could switch to Diet Pepsi. But he concluded that business was business, picked up his glass and toasted his friend. Bottoms up! "Actually," he says, "the flavor was not as objectionable as I had expected. It reminded me of chicken soup and I was almost sorry that the blood supply had vanished so quickly."

It was the right decision. His business relationship with his Chinese "blood brother" has flourished and Kaestner can't wait for his friend to visit Baltimore where he plans to treat him to raw oysters and fried soft crabs.

The Boss Isn't Always Right

Traveling with the boss can be fun. It can also be a disaster, as Shelley Mandel of St. Louis discovered when she flew with her boss to Chicago. "My boss is the one whose rental car is never there, the hotel is out of rooms, service at the restaurant is slow or his order is wrong. Fortunately I don't have the pleasure of traveling with him too often. But occasionally I do and one trip stands out in my mind."

After a long meeting in Chicago, she and the boss drove to their hotel downtown. Following a long wait in the registration line they were upgraded to a better room because of a previous bad experience the boss had had at that hotel.

"After checking into our respective rooms, we agreed to walk over to Eli's A Place for Steaks, not too far from the hotel. We were seated shortly thereafter and ordered dinner and drinks. Our drinks and salad came in a timely manner. While waiting for dinner, our waiter came out and explained that the fire alarm had gone off in the kitchen in error and fire retardant foam had bathed the entire grill, including our dinner."

Given a choice between oven cooked prime rib or a gift certificate for a free dinner in the future, Mandel would have been happy to go prime rib. But the boss insisted on heading over to one of his favorite Chicago restaurants, the Greek Islands. She suggested a cab. He preferred to drive over in the rental car.

"We walked the short distance back to the hotel and went to the parking garage. After a long wait the attendant told us they had locked the keys in the car while parking it. We were given two complimentary slices of excellent cheesecake and a free cab to the restaurant."

Don't Feel So Good Myself

A Taipei layover was just the thing for Californian Lane Johnston, enroute to a management meeting with the Australian office of his company, Stallion Technologies. But after lunch, he became ill. Luckily there was a rest stop on the highway to the airport. Everything would have gone better if someone hadn't stolen the toilet. "I looked at the hole in the floor and was sure someone had taken the toilet." Even worse, there was no toilet paper. There was a toilet paper dispenser outside. but he didn't have any Taiwanese coins. Finally a good Samaritan lent him the money he needed to buy the paper he needed.

At the airport he felt sweaty and nauseous. At least there

were Western-style toilets here. He camped out there until 15 minutes before the flight. He probably should have gone to a doctor in Taipei, but was afraid to stay. He cleaned up, straightened his suit, and brushed his hair, determined to look healthy enough to fly. Shortly after takeoff, while the seat belt sign was still on, he headed for the bathroom and stayed there for much of the next nine hours. The flight attendants took pity on him and offered their more comfortable seats, where he was able to lie down. Pepto-Bismol didn't work and Lane refused an Eastern remedy offered by a Taiwanese woman.

After landing in Brisbane he went to the emergency room where, thanks to socialized medicine, checking in was easier than renting a car. The doctors X-rayed for a kidney stone but couldn't confirm a problem. Johnston went back to his hotel, where he joined the conference. The following night, at a company dinner, one of Lane's fellow guests, a urologist, took him back to hospital. There the kidney stone was confirmed and removed two days later. By now his wife had joined him and a day after the operation they began a wonderful tour of Australia. Lane recovered quickly by not driving. Back home his insurance company and his wife's both paid in full. Johnston wound up reimbursing the companies for overpayment.

10

Sales Representatives: Life after Death

IN MY TRAVELS THREE PEOPLE, Barbara Cole, Arthur Salm and Chris Kerr, offer valuable insights on the reasons books flourish or fade. Although Cole and Salm are a continent away from Kerr, their stories provide an important link to life after the death of a salesman. They also shed light on the reasons why America's literary landscape is changing for the better.

After visiting more than 800 bookstores across the country, I'm surprised at how much more there is to learn. One of my favorite teachers is La Jolla, California's Barbara Cole. Among America's many beautiful bookstores, there's no doubt that John Cole's Book Shop wins the prize for the most dramatic setting. Located on a bluff overlooking the Pacific, the store's home is a delightful seven-room shingle building called Wisteria Cottage. This book shop is in a small park graced with sculpture, including a Henry Moore, on loan from a nearby art gallery. A walkway leads customers beneath a wisteria trellis.

Like its neighbor, the San Diego Museum of Contemporary Art, Cole's is a local landmark. While it is not the oldest bookstore in La Jolla, (that honor goes to century old Warwick's), this store has another claim to fame—Barbara Cole herself. A bookseller for 50 years, her career predates the working life of nearly every decision maker in the publishing business. There is hardly anyone in the publishing field, writer, editor or salesman, who couldn't learn a thing or two from Barbara Cole. I know I have.

When her husband died in 1959, Barbara took over the business and today she runs it in the grand manner, buying new books with the kind of care and enthusiasm you might expect from a librarian or an antiquarian collector. To have a book, any book, chosen by Barbara Cole means that you have just won a vote from someone who knows as much about the art of bookselling as anyone in America. Walking the aisles of her shop, it is obvious that she is the kind of bookseller who reads what she stocks. She listens to her customers and sells to them with the kind of enthusiasm that has created an entire generation of readers.

When I think of Barbara Cole, and I do just about each and every time I am selecting a book for publication, I think of her as one of a generation of booksellers that has made it possible for many young authors and editors to get their start. Mass production has its place, but in the world of literature each book has its own unique shape and texture, a style that reflects an author's world view. The question I often ask when looking at a manuscript is how booksellers like Barbara Cole might react to such a title. Does it have a chance with her kind of customer? If not, is there anything that can be done in the editing phase that might make this project more appealing to the serious book buyer?

By no means is Barbara Cole the only adroit bookseller in the San Diego area. I can give you a whole list of names—Susan Malk at White Rabbit, Dale Spector at Yellow Brick Road, Shirley Muller at Bay Books in Coronado, Jan Tonnesen at Wahrenbrock's Book House, Tom Stoup at Blue Door, Adrian

Newell at Warwick's, Carole Carden at Esmeralda Book and Coffee, Joe Zangoro at the Book Loft—who offer the same kind of experience and professionalism. And like each of them, Cole is dedicated to bringing in the best books she can find from any source. She makes her decisions after carefully reviewing each sales rep's presentation and sizing up their enthusiasm for the best and brightest frontlist. Quaint is the word for Cole's, which does not own a computerized inventory system. In fact it doesn't even keep a card file on its stock list. "We use the eyeball inventory system," Cole says with a big laugh, seated at her desk in the middle of the art book department.

Although the store is strong on hardcovers, Cole's shop also has a good selection of trade paperbacks. Art, literature, history, science, children's books, these are just a few of the categories that she highlights, sometimes at the expense of certain commercial bestsellers that may not be a good match for her clientele. She also skips most business, sports and computer books.

In a region that has no shortage of discount stores, Barbara Cole doesn't cut prices on her new titles, even carefully selected bestselling authors like Stephen King. "New people come to us after visiting our competition in the shopping centers and they ask: 'Are you really charging full price?' But most of our old customers are faithful to us. They appreciate our selection and service."

It's not hard to understand why. Exploring the nooks and crannies of her shop, you won't find a coffee bar or run into a costumed children's book character like Barney. The closest thing she has to sidelines are a world music CD rack and a small harmonica shop run by her grandson down on the ground floor. Full-page ads bannering big discounts beneath headlines proclaiming that "Books Cost Too Much," and other popular techniques used by large stores to promote their books are not part of Cole's marketing strategy.

"Our approach is really rather simple. We meet with sales reps who help us go through lengthy catalogs and pick out the best books for our store. Since they've read the forthcoming titles, I rely heavily on their judgment and enthusiasm when making my own decisions. If an experienced sales rep who knows our store is excited about a new title we'll probably take it. In many instances they persuade us to buy books we would have never considered."

This direct relationship between seller and buyer is vital in the world of children's books. Like most experienced buyers, Barbara Cole wants to read books for young people, particularly picture books, before committing. "The Harcourt Brace rep was just here," she said pointing to a canvas bag full of new titles and galleys. "They presented the adult list and dropped off the kid's books for me to look through. They'll be back in a couple days to take my order for children's books."

Regular sales rep visits are crucial to Barbara Cole because she is constantly on the lookout for the unique and the unusual, especially the larger book that her competitors are unlikely to offer. A good example is Rien Poortvliet's *Noah's Ark,* a wonderful art book from Harry Abrams. "This has been a big one for us and we might have never carried it if it weren't for their rep. We also do well with Thames and Hudson, Rizzoli and many smaller presses that aren't catering to the discount stores."

While others agonize about the future of publishing, Cole approaches her days much as she has for the past 50 years. "The business has changed," she says, "that's for sure. There are more stores than there used to be. More books are being published. And there are definitely more readers."

Then why are there so many gloomy stories about the decline

of book sales, even though dollar volume sales continue to increase? Why is there such a focus on big publishers losing market share and cutting their lists?

"You can spend a lot of money on fixtures and displays, charge publishers extra fees to display their books prominently, advertise like crazy, get people into your stores and still not sell them anything," says Cole.

"Selling books takes a lot of practice. Customers expect a lot. You've got to have what your customers expect and you have to get it quickly. Otherwise they'll pass you by. A lot of our business is generated by customers who went looking for a book at a bigger store and couldn't find it. The clerk will look it up on the computer and declare that it's out of print. Often that's not true. The problem is that the book hasn't arrived yet from the big company's central warehouse. The same customer will call us and discover we've already got it.

"A good book does find its way to its clientele. That's why sales reps are invaluable, they make sure we have the books they know, based on years of experience, are going to be in demand thanks to favorable reviews. And if we don't have it, or have run out, we know how to get another copy in a day or two, which is not true at big stores that tend to be slower on special orders.

"One of my favorite rep stories comes from a man in Los Angeles who got a call from an author complaining that his book wasn't in stock at a local chain. The rep suggested the author meet him at the shop. At the sales counter a clerk carefully explained that the book was unavailable. The rep turned to an adjacent shelf and pulled down five copies. Frankly, we tend to be a little less computerized and a little more organized which explains why the reps like us."

Despite the store's long tenure, Barbara Cole has discovered that even she has been downgraded by a few of her largest and oldest vendors. Shortly after Cole's 50th anniversary, both Simon and Schuster's adult trade division and HarperCollins pulled their sales reps from her account.

"It's hard enough to buy books when you're working your way through a long list like this one with a rep," she says holding up a stack of HarperCollins catalogs. "I know there are titles in here that I would have ordered based on my old rep's recommendations. But now I don't have the benefit of her experience, based on her reading of an advance copy. I won't have all the details on tours and publicity as well as titles that might have special relevance to an English professor at the University of California or a research biologist in the Salk Institute. I'm sorry to say that on some of these titles I'm in the dark. The catalog doesn't give me enough information to make informed buying decisions on this vast list. Obviously I'll be ordering less books this season from HarperCollins."

It's easy for the adult trade book division of HarperCollins or Simon and Schuster to make a case against calling on Barbara Cole. Apparently her recent orders were not large enough to justify a rep's time. But as a publisher who sells to her, one book at a time, I can vouch for her integrity, her creditworthiness and the fact that she holds on to her books patiently, knowing that a well stocked store is its own best advertisement. Like San Francisco's City Lights and other literary bookstores around the country such as Von's in West Lafayette, Indiana, and Oblong Books in Millertown, New York, she understands that while quality books may take a little longer to sell they build the store's reputation and clientele. A customer who finds a unique book is likely to come back for more recommendations. This trust between publisher, bookseller and customer is the heart of a long term business relationship.

Although I have had many wonderful visits to San Diego over the years, none can match the excitement and sense of discovery that comes from a tour of the community's bookshops. Indeed I can't think of a better way to get in touch with the spirit of a new town than to visit its local bookstores and chat with the owners who know so much about the literary life of their city. From the first grader picking out a picture book to a grandparent looking for a gift book, there is an integrity and sense of purpose about these shops. The thought that this universe is somehow shrinking, that an industry producing an astonishing 40,000 books a year is a candidate for dismemberment is ridiculous.

Shortly before I left Barbara Cole's store she told me Harper Collins and Simon and Schuster were making a mistake when they decided to take her store off the rep list. This view was shared by Arthur Salm, the book editor at the *San Diego Union,* one of only nine dailies in our country to publish a freestanding Sunday book review. "I think Barbara Cole is on to something," he told me while showing some of the 200 books sent to his office for review consideration each week.

"Every time I pick up one of these titles," he told me in his office, "I can feel the author on one side of me and the publisher on the other. Although some of the books are sent to other sections for feature coverage, I have to reject books every day that are absolutely worthy of review space. With a few exceptions like a new Pynchon novel, you could take out every single book we're reviewing this week and put together another section filled with reviews of equally worthy titles. I feel terrible that we can't cover all the books that deserve space. I feel terrible when I meet an author of a book I couldn't review because we had to give our space to another equally deserving author. If the day comes when I don't feel terrible about this, I'd be completely surprised.

"There's been a lot of talk about publishers selling out. But it isn't really true. A few years back a magazine writer went back and read all the bestsellers in the '40s and found there was just as much commercial shlock on the list then as there is today."

What has changed, Salm suggests, is the fact that some large publishers have lost patience with the traditional idea of nurturing a new author. "There was a time when a house would go with a new author on the idea that she could become the next Alice Hoffman. They would publish one book, then another, get good reviews and make a commitment to the writer's career. The idea was that perhaps in a few years they would make a little money or maybe break even. In any case her work would help attract other authors to the company and boost the list.

"Now there is more of a blockbuster mentality that belies some of the fundamentals of publishing. Expectations are higher. The theory in Hollywood has been that you spend $300 million on three films and hope one of them takes off. Despite what some publishers think, you can't treat books the way you treat movies, dumping them if they don't make their first weekend gross revenue projections. Now even Hollywood is getting the message. That's why you are seeing a lot more small films being produced. The studios understand that lower budget films, Sundance Film Festival winners for example, can break out if you give them a little time to find their natural audience."

Even with these changes there is no way to compare the film business, which releases about 300 titles per year, with the 40,000 title a year book business. "Let's face it, when a new film or play comes to town it gets reviewed," says Salm. "Unfortunately it's only possible to cover a small fraction of the new books being released. Every week it's triage in my department, deciding which books to review. It certainly is easier to make money publishing a couple of bestsellers than to divide your attention across a much broader list of books. And this explains why so many books get short shrift in publishing houses that are not run by book people."

If the blockbuster approach is not giving publishers the results they expect, what is a reasonable alternative? The answer is based on the reasonable assumption that books have a future. I remember Apple Computer's Steve Jobs, years before the company he helped create was downsizing, predicting that the book would be replaced by a hand held computer. The idea was that Chaucer on a chip could be inserted into the device just like a Game Boy cartridge. No one bought it. For all their problems, book publishers are doing considerably better these days than Apple. In fact, one of the most profitable sectors is the publishing of heavy, expensive tomes designed to help computer users figure out how to make the machines work.

"In 200 years," says Salm, "if people are still reading, and I think they will be, books will still be around. There's no other format that can match it for convenience and portability. Books are just ideal."

While many other media compete directly against books, it's encouraging that the publishing industry remains considerably larger than the movie business. And even at a time when a number of the largest publishing houses are stagnating or in decline, many newly organized companies are flourishing. Some publishers have discovered it is difficult to computerize matters of taste. Like movie producers, who make *Batman 3* on the assumption that it will perform as well as *Batman 1* or *2*, publishers know last year's success can be this year's failure.

Dennis Rodman's first book succeeded, not because he was a literary giant, but because a lot of people wanted to read about an eccentric basketball star—once. His second book bombed, even Oprah's show canceled him, perhaps because the reading public learned what it needed from his first title.

As a beginning book publisher I have learned you don't need a superstar author to break in. It's even possible to sell books to people who have never heard of you. The trick is to make sure that the people who buy your books actually pay for them. This is harder than it looks, as many publishers will quickly explain when they are presenting royalty statements yielding nothing to the author. The reason is that books aren't really sold, they are consigned to stores that can return them if they don't find a buyer at the retail level. The euphemistic word "sell through" refers to books that are actually sold and paid for by stores, as opposed to those that are dead on arrival, because they remain unsold and not paid for. When things are going badly it's possible for 30 percent to 50 percent of a publisher's books to be returned, sometimes even more. In fact, many big publishers will actually pay stores not to return books. At one point in 1997 books by President Clinton, Pope John Paul and Oprah Winfrey were all in this shared markdown category, meaning that booksellers were given huge discounts by publishers to substantially reduce the price of these titles and in the case of Winfrey, actually give the book away with the purchase of another bestselling title she wrote.

One reason this happens is that publishers overprint their bestsellers to make sure their customers don't run out. Given the economies of scale, there are worse things than taking a couple of hundred thousand returns on a book that might sell a million copies. Unfortunately it doesn't always work this way, particularly when wholesale outlets sticker bestsellers at a price below the wholesale price charged many bookstores. With customers shifting their purchases to these off-price mass merchants, the publishers find, inevitably, that their books don't sell well in bookstores. This leads to the shared markdown (both the publisher and bookseller reduce their price) that allows retail stores to cut their prices to offer the same discounts found at warehouse clubs like Costco or Sam's Club. All of this is proof positive of the maxim that "we lose money on every copy but make it up on volume."

I found it ironic that in bookstore after bookstore owners had few, if any copies of the *New York Times* bestseller that were stacked up in the warehouse emporiums. Unable to compete on price, these stores had shifted their buying to the kinds of titles that are not sold at a deep discount nearby. A healthy mix of literature and children's books, local interest titles, small and university press titles as well as an emphasis on books from seasons past, referred to in the trade as backlist, makes it easier for these shops to carve out a niche. In a word they create their own bestsellers. And, of course, they do find that certain kinds of literary titles perform well because of their absence in the chains. Diane Sullivan, at Wind and Tide Bookshop in Oak Harbor, Washington, told me an all-too-typical story of a customer who was on the fence about a new Alice Hoffman novel. After waiting for some weeks, she finally came in to buy the book.

"I guess Costco isn't going to carry this one at a big discount," she said while paying for the hardcover at this lovely Whidbey Island store. Obviously independent stores like Wind and Tide are very interested in the works of smaller publishing houses that do not undercut their customers. As Tom Lowry of Lowry's Bookstore in Three Rivers, Michigan, explained to me: "When Wal-Mart called and asked me if I wanted to take out a membership in Sam's Club, I asked the solicitor, 'Why the hell would I want to do that? You guys are trying to put me out of business.'"

Who then is going to correct the imbalance between good books and the reading public. Certainly not the warehouse chain or the largest publishing companies ratcheting down their sales forces. One possibility is a new breed of sales rep who really believes there is life after the death of a salesman.

In some instances their careers parallel the industry's fortunes. An example is New Yorker Chris Kerr who cut his teeth in the '70s as international sales manager for Harcourt Brace. He decided to leave after learning that the company was moving its offices to a new building in San Diego Sea World's parking lot. A young man not eager to move west, he found a new job—opening a New York office for Basil Blackwell Ltd., a British academic publisher.

Kerr ran the entire show out of his Brooklyn apartment. "I'd convinced them that I could persuade the largest national account, B. Dalton, to buy the list without the slightest idea of how to do it. In addition to Blackwell's pressure, the family assigned one of their sons, a former British Army office in Northern Ireland, to intern with B. Dalton. He would be there to watch me tank.

"At the time, I was doing everything on no money and made reservations with People Express. In those days you took everything you could for a chain presentation, all the way up to a life-size inflatable doll of the top author. But I knew that it wasn't going to work. I was selling academic titles to a mass-market chain. By the time we took off on my first big sales trip, I was in meltdown."

When the plane flew into an electrical storm and lost its navigational equipment, the pilot announced that the flight was returning to Newark. There, Kerr boarded another plane and flew to Minneapolis without any of his luggage or presentation materials. After checking into a two-story cinderblock motel, Kerr hung his khakis and shirt in the bathroom and turned on the shower, hoping the steam would remove some of the wrinkles. Then he sat down and tried to reconstruct his presentation.

At 2 A.M. the front desk woke Kerr to explain that his shower was leaking into the room below. The rep walked through scalding water to unplug the overflowing tub. Then he headed for the hallway, which was completely flooded. The rest of the night was spent working on his presentation. On checkout the following morning the clerk said: "Are you the guy in room 312? You just missed the guy in room 212 who had a white jacket stained red by the dye from your carpet that dripped through the ceiling."

At B. Dalton, a dazed Kerr met with buyer Mike Heiny and presented a German history title. The buyer reached up to his shelf and pulled down a copy. "I know this book is really wonderful. The reason I know is that I've bought it and read it." Kerr gulped. "Blackwell hadn't bothered to tell me that they had already sold this title's paperback rights to New York University Press."

During much of Kerr's career, reps were central to the marketing strategy of the large publishing houses. It wasn't uncommon for companies like Random House to send as many as four different sales people to a single independent store. When I started my company, a bookseller down the street from my current office complained about Random House devoting too much attention to his store. He had a very hard time justifying all day appointments. The company's long list was split between red and blue sales forces, while a third team would handle distributed lines such as Sierra Club Books and Shambhala. In addition, Random House Value Publishing would offer remainders and bargain priced collections. There was also a juvenile rep.

Similarly, a company like Macmillan with its vast list of reference titles ranging from the Arthur Frommer guidebook line to business books would send reps far and wide to show the company's colors and handle customer-service issues such as cooperative advertising, author tours and special discounts.

But as many of these companies have consolidated or downsized their sales forces, many stores have discovered their twice-a-year visit by a veteran rep (including lunch) was replaced by a phone call from a telemarketer in New York. In more remote areas some stores suddenly found their annual visit replaced with a mere catalog. Many road warriors were also taken off their traditional territories to focus on large national accounts that included mass merchants treating books as a sideline.

Kerr, who moved on to Little Brown before leaving in the spring of 1997 to represent 20 independent publishers through a partnership called Parson Weems, says: "New Jersey is part of my mid-Atlantic territory. Stores that used to see four Random House reps a year were suddenly seeing none. This was a little weird since New Jersey is in New York's backyard. It's a place where a lot of authors live, as do many journalists, publishers and agents. Getting books into community bookstores here is important. Even though these shops are a short drive or train ride from the publishing houses themselves, the neighborhood shops are getting short shrift or being ignored. If these publishers can't get a rep to New Jersey, you can imagine what's happening in upstate New York or Maine. You've got a lot of quality bookstores that just aren't getting the attention they deserve from large houses."

Kerr thinks downsizing is a mistake. "There's been a lot written about the diminishing role of the independent bookstore. But I still think the local community store remains at the heart and soul of retail. When I was sales manager at Little Brown, we handled one of the top New York publishing houses, Warner Books. I was the guy who turned to Warner boss Larry Kirshbaum, and told him it was time to stop flogging a certain new novel. For nine months he had gotten up every single morning thinking of new ways to sell this book. And he tried everything, tours, ads, publicity, you name it.

"We'd do things like drive a galley of the book out to key independent shops such as Warren Cassell's mostly hardcover shop, Just Books, in Greenwich, Connecticut. Warren is the kind of local bookseller who can help put a new novel on the map, give it the visibility it needs to get a healthy start."

All this was frustrating. "The book was going nowhere.... I told Larry it was time to let it rest."

But the publisher hung in, long after others lost heart. Little Brown reps made pitches to key independent accounts, dropping off galleys wherever they could. Cassell sold over 1,000 copies. His success and that of similar independents around the country started putting the book on local bestseller lists. Larger stores picked up on the title and *The Bridges of Madison County* went on to sell millions of copies in hardcover, becoming one of the most successful novels of the '90s.

"Nearly every publisher can point to local stores that have jumped on a promising new title and sold it into the hundreds, and in some cases, thousands," adds Kerr. "This has certainly been true in my own case. And when I look at these success stories, nearly every one of them began with one of our employees visiting the store to present the book."

Despite this fact of publishing life, many of the nation's

leading independents, shops that anchor their community's literary scene, find they are getting short shrift. Consider the two Books and Books stores in Coral Gables and Miami Beach. A key stop on any Florida author tour, the Coral Gables store features as many as two readings a day during peak season. Shops with deep backlist, they are a publisher's dream. Owner Mitchell Kaplan is also a key figure on the board of the Miami Book Fair, a wildly successful community event that brings celebrity authors and promising newcomers to town each fall.

You can imagine how Kaplan felt when he learned, along with the majority of independent bookstores around the country, that his store was no longer eligible to buy direct from Macmillan Publishing. In the summer of 1997, this large imprint canceled the direct accounts at Books and Books and every other bookstore ordering less than $10,000 worth of stock annually. No longer eligible to buy books direct at discounts up to 47 percent off list price, these customers would now have to turn to wholesalers who typically sell at a 40 to 42 percent discount.

Losing these discount points is particularly difficult at lucrative author events, where stores like to buy books direct to maximize their profit margins. Obviously if a major author like Arthur Frommer is going to sell 200 copies of a book at a signing, the extra 7 percent could add up to hundreds of dollars. How did Kaplan, a major customer for Frommer books and other Macmillan Publishing titles, feel about losing the ability to buy direct?

"Not very good," he said. "The fact that we spend less than $10,000 a year with this company doesn't mean we're a small customer. I just pulled all my Macmillan Publishing titles, particularly the Frommer line, and I'm sending them back. I am going to demand a check; it will be thousands of dollars.

"The whole industry is in a kind of a crisis," he told me. "The larger publishers as well as small presses are very insecure. All of this insecurity has its roots in the last five years with the growth of the corporate store and the diminished influence of the independent bookseller."

Not being able to buy direct from a major publisher undercuts the ability of stores to make extra dollars on key lines, money that could be used to nurture promising new authors and represent special interest titles that may take awhile to reach their natural audience. Many of the booksellers who promote these books bring great enthusiasm to their calling. A good example is Easy Going, a Berkeley, California, bookshop. One of their most popular visiting authors has been Arthur Frommer, who appeared at the store on four different occasions. "Even though we spend $8,000 a year with Macmillan, we can no longer get his books direct," owner Thelma Elkins told me. "What's even worse is that to reestablish a direct account with Macmillan we have to give them a $25,000 opening order. This is customer relations?"

Several months after I spoke with Kaplan and Elkins, Macmillan Publishing announced a change of heart and agreed to let stores open accounts with a $10,000 order.

Chris Kerr believes that Macmillan Publishing, like many big companies, is trying to respond to the marketplace. The problem is they are not sure exactly how to do it. "The large publishers cutting back on house rep calls at local stores are behind the times. All the attention focused on mass merchants belies the fact that many of the strongest book buying areas are ideal for small entrepreneurial businesses.

"There are still many communities across America where people like to park and walk to half a dozen merchants. These shops represent a vital link to customers. Many already enjoy close relationships with authors. They are much more aggressive about reaching into their communities. They contact schools and local businesses, organize book fairs, special events, charitable programs, media events, anything that will spread the love of reading. If they can hang in there, they will do significantly better in the years ahead."

Kerr believes that independent stores, with their strong customer base, owner-operators and relatively low operating costs, are in a much stronger position that some of their larger customers who aren't dependent on books for their livelihood.

"The mass merchant has an ambivalent attitude toward books. A Costco or Sam's Club is essentially selling books at cost, or in some cases below cost when you add in freight and handling. If these books don't produce any profit, what is their value to the store? The answer is simple. Books are one of the few categories where you can replenish with new product any time. That's why they are displayed on the front tables where they sell staggering numbers. They're terrific window dressing in a store where customers are looking for something new amidst the same old cartons of milk, toilet tissue and dog food.

"Let's face it, books have a halo effect. When I started out as a salesman, my first job was working for a distributor of small presses from Britain. People were very polite and supportive. A little while later I was hired by Oxford University Press and instantly people's assessment of me changed. Overnight my IQ had gone up by 25 percent. People treated me as if I had read the entire 10,000 title backlist. Books do bestow a certain respectability and dignity on the enterprise, even though you might never open the covers. There's that wonderful passage in *The Great Gatsby* where he didn't crack the spines because he knew the books were there as decor. For many of these corporate discount stores books are there for decoration.

"The smaller, personal booksellers have become even more valuable because they have the ability to impart some life into this mix. Sales reps are also crucial because stores need them to select what is valuable on a publisher's lists. Our recommendations carry more weight than they ever have. That's why independent reps and the surviving house reps are in demand. You can always tell when a good sales rep has been in the store. It is reflected in the variety of the books that you find there. These shops are more alert to the quirky title. They can differentiate themselves from the homogenizers down the street. They are doing double duty to find not only the legitimately marketable and commercial but also set out books that are touchstones of their individuality and originality.

"Reps don't just *schlep* books. They are taking stock, negotiating with the credit manager and bartering with publicity people for author appearances. What the stores are really saying to us is 'rhetoric and advertising hype aside, is this something for us.' If you want to get back in you better be pretty solid."

Those reps who are willing to seduce the stores abandoned by larger publishers are well received. "There's a fabulous collection of university and specialist and museum stores who have been abandoned by publishers. They have really been left to their own devices and they are really annoyed. This change means we get more airtime and a better reception. You can't browbeat people to try things they don't want to try. Every time another big publisher cuts its rep force or consolidates territories and lines, the more opportunity there is for us.

"My little business is a beneficiary of that rollback. Fully two-thirds of the publishers my company represents had reps, gave up, tried telemarketing and other strategies and then went back to reps. These days our biggest virtue is not our cleverness but the fact that we show up."

11

The Book Business: A Shelf Game

RAPOPORT'S FIRST LAW: The success of a salesman correlates directly to the distance from the customer's front door. Corollary: Any CEO that is not spending at least 100 hours a year inside the stores of his customers, big and small, is a good candidate for early retirement, perhaps as early as yesterday. Now let's saddle up and find out what the traveling salesmen is up against in a country where Main Street has become a theme park.

One of the great myths of *fin de siècle* capitalism is that small retail is on the skids. It is true that small stores, not just bookstores, are closing in many parts of the country. Some were my customers and I miss them. It is also true that Montgomery Ward filed for bankruptcy protection in the summer of 1997, as Macy's did a few years earlier, along with many other large retailers. New bookstores, both independents and chains, are opening across the country. Today nearly 30,000 bookstores are in business and they create an impressive retailing panorama.

The pattern is typical. Entrepreneurs come up with a new product and get it off the ground. Long before the chain stores and department stores were carrying home computers, it was local community-based computer stores that provided the products, the service and the support necessary to launch the industry. Large electronics chains and department stores were not able to fully capitalize on this trend until after the ground-work had been carefully laid by thousands of independent merchants, many of them family businesses. I doubt that even the largest computer retailers could have made it were it not for the fact that local stores educated a whole generation of computer users.

Even after the larger retail corporations begin to edge out smaller competitors, independent stores remain viable. On my travels across America I find locally owned bookstores open-ing in every section of the country. A lot of lip service is paid to the success of specialty retail like travel or New Age book-stores. But it is also true that many experienced business peo-ple are opening small general bookstores in communities ranging from Colfax, California, to Norwell, Massachusetts. In some cases these stores function as community centers, a place where you can get a latte, a muffin, a newspaper and a book, an update of the old newsstand where customers bought mass paperbacks, cigarettes and their favorite newspaper. The big change is obvious. Instead of taking the word of a distrib-utor who is pushing the latest gaggle of mass market romance, western, crime and pop fiction into racks at drug and grocery stores, customers find their reading material at stores where it's possible to sit a spell and have an espresso. Larger stores are also opening in places like Scottsdale, Arizona, and Bakers-field, California. Also, many stores are expanding in locations like Madison, Connecticut, and Terre Haute, Indiana.

The shelf life of books sold in these new bookstore/cafes is much longer than the mass market outlet where books are selected by corporations who have literally leased rack space. Mass-market books that don't sell in a few weeks at a supermarket or drug store chain are pulled from the racks and stripped of their covers, which are sent back for publisher credit. The covers are proof that the book wasn't sold. The books themselves are then pulped. A New York publisher told me a few years back that it's possible to make money if just 25 percent of the books printed sell. Even with this kind of margin many publishers are reducing mass-market titles such as romance and westerns and concentrating instead on trade paperbacks (you're holding one).

Given a choice, many customers will spend an extra $5 or $6 for a trade paperback. To begin with, there is broader selection on the trade paperback side. Publishers tend to limit the number of new mass market titles because of the high number of sales needed to justify their publication and make money. While many of these books do perform well in high-traffic locations, the overall sales have been disappointing in recent years. Customers are reshaping the market and quality is winning out over quantity.

Another current trend is market cannibalization. Large publishers try to sell their books everywhere. Titles once found primarily in bookstores are now found in every manner of chain and variety store, often at significant discounts. Books are overpublished, overdistributed, underbought and inevitably returned in excessive numbers. So-called bestsellers sometimes fizzle, to the disappointment of all concerned.

Some of the discount mass merchants ordering these bestselling titles only carry a limited number of books, relying on low prices to make up for the poor selection. These stores skim off bestseller sales from bookstores. Stores dedicated to selling these heavily promoted titles don't have the cash flow to keep them in stock. If they start slowly, which is often the case for titles that take time to generate word of mouth and favorable reviews, the books are returned quickly. The shortening of inventory time—bookstores returning books to generate a credit they can use to barter on other titles—hurts everyone, especially the reading public. Some publishers, to protect themselves, lean toward quick turning books that are easily promoted via celebrities, news events, film or television dramatizations. A good example is the O.J. collected works, born and bred on television with every angle a publisher could dream of: sports, sex, murder, mayhem, the race card and, of course, the inevitable judicial circus.

But what about books that might take two, three, five, even 20 years to finally reach their natural audience, thanks, say, to the penultimate Oprah Book Club selection. These books, the ones that might truly stand the test of time, are harder for large publishers to produce and sell for the following reasons:

1. No one has ever heard of the author.

2. The author is unlikely to command review or media space.

3. The sales reps are required to sell the book before they've been given an advance copy to read.

4. Stores with limited budgets are unlikely to stock the book in sufficient numbers to justify a print run that covers the publisher's substantial overhead.

5. Due to tax laws, publishers can't write off the printing bill for unsold copies until the book is declared out of print, meaning customers can no longer order the title.

Is it any wonder that large publishers are shrinking their lists to focus on what the head of HarperCollins calls a few key books in the top categories. In many cases most of the marketing money is committed to these books before they are even written. Relatively few books outside of children's publishing are field tested through advance reading copies.

If you believe, as I do, that much of what's right with our country began with a good book, then I hope you'll consider what's at stake here. We're talking about much more than the economic destiny of a few thousand booksellers and publishers or the writing careers of the 40,000 authors behind each year's crop of new books. The real issue is whether any of us will be able to go into a bookstore 10 years from now and find books that break new ground. Or will the authors, publishers and stores be forced to find another way to present the kinds of ideas that separate our culture from those where private libraries are the province of the rich, where publishing is not a right but a government monopoly and where books that speak the truth are destroyed to prevent them from reaching people who need to read them?

Censorship is more than just government abuse of First Amendment rights. Equally powerful and just as frightening is the self-censorship created when bad work forces out the good, where new ideas can't reach the public because they don't sell as well as old ideas and of course, where the public is not given a meaningful choice. In their attempted monopolization of mass-market distribution, a handful of publishing companies have succeeded in reducing the market for their own goods. When publishers insist that the audience for their products is in decline, that it's not their fault, that the public isn't reading as much as they used to, they are simply refusing to acknowledge statistics that show higher library circulation, higher school enrollments, higher readership and, of course, higher book sales in many categories.

The only reason more good books are failing to reach more readers is the self-defeating way many large publishers go about their business. The fact is that everywhere you look in America new stores are being opened. In Muskegon, Michigan, four hours drive from Chicago, there were no bookstores when I was in high school 35 years ago. Today this same community has four bookstores and three others can be found within a 15-minute drive. Within an hour's drive are two outstanding children's bookstores, and one, Pooh's Corner in Holland, Michigan, is a beauty with impressive five-foot-tall spines of children's classics bordering the entryway.

By the time I began making my first sales calls to bookstores, I had written or co-authored 15 books, worked for another publisher, made more than 100 bookstore appearances, edited and packaged many books for other publishing companies. But it was only when I began visiting stores with my sample case that I began to understand the difference between marketing and sales. Marketing is what they teach in business school; selling is the work that begins when the customer says "no" or "not now" or "we'll get back to you."

The Travel Game

In the mind of almost every customer, there are three questions: How long will this take? How much will it cost? How quickly can I get back to work? Selling, even when everything is going perfectly, is a disruption of a customer's life. I wouldn't agree with those who say the customer is always right, but I do believe that the customer is always in a hurry.

So, of course, am I. When I began making sales calls in my own neighborhood and at large trade shows, it was obvious that selling was a focused activity. But as I began making long plane, rail and car trips to other parts of the country I also learned that the clock is a salesman's greatest enemy. Getting lost, stuck in traffic, being held up because a customer is late, weather problems, misplacing luggage, these are the challenges that make the difference between success and failure.

Packing is one of the trickiest problems. The issue is not clothes, it's what's inside your sample case. Most sales training focuses on technique, not the product, yet this is precisely where many traveling salesmen get into trouble. Carrying the wrong products to the wrong market is one of the easiest ways to have a fruitless visit. This is a particularly difficult problem for book salesmen since buying patterns can shift neighborhood by neighborhood. A buyer at a Tower Books store in Sacramento mentioned to me once that his stock was vastly different from another company store just two miles away.

One of the first things I and most salesman do when visiting a store is to check it out to see what sort of books work best in that environment. As I show my books, I explain to the owner where they might fit on the shelf and which customers are most likely to purchase them. Here's an example. Over the past few years many of my customers have succeeded with a book called *Get Out of My Life, but First Could You Drive Me and Cheryl to the Mall?* We publish a book with similar appeal, Gina Davidson's *Treasure,* which focuses on a single mother and her 13-year-old daughter. Because both these titles are favored by parents of teenagers, I suggest stores place them side by side. Obviously the customer who enjoyed the first book is likely to have fun with the second.

Technically, *Treasure* is a backlist title, meaning it was published several years ago. Most sales representatives visit each store two to three times a year, focusing on key front list titles about to be published, as well as selected backlist that is a good candidate for reorder. Because we don't have a national sales force, about 90 percent of my calls are made on stores that have never seen our list before. As a result, all our books, even those published several years back, are new to buyers looking hard for titles they can handsell in respectable numbers—good

books that have not been preempted by the discount chains.

For this strategy to work we have to go far beyond the typical store visited by the average publishing sales representative. Big publishers can only afford to send reps to larger stores that will write orders large enough to justify the expense of a sales call. Because I'm the owner, my cost of sales is lower. I can happily afford to call on a promising small store that would slip below the radar of a large publishing company or a sales rep handling a group of small presses.

These small businesses compete in fascinating ways. Consider one of my customers, H&B Book Store and Mattress Outlet located next door to Wal-Mart in Columbia City, Indiana. Ginger Bellam and her partner Rene Walker originally ran their shop as a small bookstore. Two years ago Ginger's brother, Richard Hauser, decided to combine his mattress outlet with the bookstore location. "It's kind of funny how it works out," she explained. "Some people come in here looking for a book and wind up buying a bed. Another plus is that the sales cycles of the two products complement each other. At Christmas time, when mattress sales are soft," she explained, "book sales are brisk. And when book sales taper off during the early part of the year, beds do well."

"One of the biggest mistakes a retailer can make," says Ginger with a nod toward Wal-Mart next door, "is to try to compete with everyone. There's no point in our trying to charge less than they do. What we do is carry the books people really want to buy, which may explain why Wal-Mart employees come over here to buy our books on their lunch hour. Also, Wal-Mart doesn't have much in the way of beds, unless you want something really cheap. As a result, after people have been disappointed by their selection, it's easy for them to come next door and buy from us."

With an Oprah Book Club, a nice selection of humor, romance and used titles, the store manages to offer a cross-section of popular fiction, bestsellers and kid's books that aren't easy to find elsewhere in town. This store full of sleepers also is a good place to find books on kings like Elvis or queens like Elizabeth II. The store also does a strong special-order business thanks to fast wholesaler service. Usually customers can get the books they need within two or three days. While this is a small store, it does manage to provide the community with titles that are not always immediately available at the library or Wal-Mart-type stores that select their titles for a national audience.

One of the things H&B does not try to be is a prototype for anyone else. And this is precisely the point. "Because we are not trying to compete with anyone else, we are free to operate the store the way we want. That's the biggest mistake you can make, trying to copy someone down the street because they are bigger than you are," Ginger says.

12

Short Subjects II

Stockings to Go

WHEN SHE WAS WORKING for the Population Institute, a Los Angeles based family planning organization, Kathy Goldmark enlisted the help of rock stars to spread her message. Slightly ahead of her time, she handed out condoms at rock and roll conventions in the mid-'70s and even dispensed poetry known as "condom couplets." Traveling as a single woman, the weirdest things would happen. "If you walked into a restaurant by yourself, people would just assume you were a hooker. I was young and didn't look like a business person. Most of the difficulties and misunderstandings were about my age and the fact that I was a woman. People didn't expect you to be serious or smart. On one flight an older man struck up a conversation. 'I see you wear fishnet stockings. What kind do you like?' I was trying to answer him politely, but after a few minutes of this I was about to hit the stewardess button and ask to be moved to another seat. Turned out he was the regional sales manager for Hanes and after the flight he sent me more stuff than I could imagine."

An Ill Wind

When he served as vice president for information systems of a southeastern U.S. commercial bank, Jack Grantham was sent to Omaha, Nebraska, for four days to train on a credit card system his employer wanted to purchase. On the first day of class, at an office building alongside an Omaha highway, everyone watched the sky grow pitch black.

Lines of cars jammed the freeway. The sky became so dark that the instructor left to check on weather conditions. Within minutes most of the class had disappeared. In the hall several people shouted that it was time to head for the basement. On the lower level the entire class was sipping power drinks at the health club. It was Wednesday, Ladies Day.

"As I was offered a free drink, a 'freight train' sound accompanied by crashing heavy objects, wind and breaking glass confirmed the obvious. A tornado had just hit the classroom building. It was lights out and after the screaming ended some of the ladies lit candles. A double funnel cloud had jumped a hill just behind the building, hit the other end and continued across the highway to devastate part of Omaha. I found later that the windows on my rental car had exploded and a 2x4 had shot through one of the tires. Half of the classroom building was destroyed. We managed our way through the rest of the day in survival mode and returned to our home town the next day." This rude interruption of the training program made no difference because Grantham's bank chose not to purchase the credit card system.

A Key Breakdown

Cary Lindsay of The Woodlands, Texas, was in Spokane, Washington, when he found that he needed to meet with a sales rep in Walla Walla. At the airport the following morning he learned his short commuter flight might be diverted to Yakima because of bad weather. The sole passenger aboard, he was told by the pilot 20 minutes after takeoff that the plane was, indeed, going to Yakima. Because of airport closures in Seattle, Portland and Boise, the Yakima field was jammed with diverted flights. Unable to make his appointment in Walla Walla, he rented a car and drove back to Seattle to catch a flight to San Francisco.

"At the rental counter the very friendly and cordial lady informed me that she had gone out and driven the car to the nearby exit door, scraped the ice off the window and left the motor running to keep the vehicle warm. This was a customer-oriented agent who should be commended for her assistance to a stranded airline passenger."

The trip to Seattle was a breeze. "I arrived at Sea-Tac Airport with about 30 minutes before my scheduled departure. I pulled into the rental return area and stopped my vehicle in the assigned space. I reached down to turn off the ignition and much to my surprise I gripped a key chain that had to be the biggest in the world and to my amazement it was filled with car keys. I had been so busy trying to make it to Seattle that I didn't realize the agent had given me her master key ring.

I gathered my luggage and walked into the return counter and started to say, 'I just drove a car in from Yak ...' when the agent blurted out: 'You are the fellow we have been looking for! You have all the keys for every rental car in Yakima. We haven't been able to rent a car there because you have all the keys.'"

Your Luggage Is Missing

Scott Blanch, who lives in San Diego, knows his way around baggage claims departments. On a flight for Motorola from Amsterdam to Los Angeles he checked his carry-on bag with

KLM. "What could happen on a direct flight?"

Plenty, as it turns out. When he arrived at the L.A. airport, Blanch was given a small bag that had been inside his carry-on. What had happened to the rest of his belongings? The airline said they had been destroyed and bought him a new carry-on. He lost his best suit as well as expensive gifts that were not easily replaceable. Four days later the airline sent a delivery-man to his house with the missing bag, demanding delivery payment. His wife refused to pay. That was his last trip on KLM.

Another time, in Phoenix for a connecting flight, Blanch checked his luggage with Northwest for a trip to Taipei. The bag never arrived. A month later, after returning home, the airline called with good news. They had found his luggage, cracked but intact. Nothing was missing. It was great. Blanch didn't even have to pack for his next trip. He just picked up the luggage at the airport, boarded his flight and returned to Taipei.

On a trip to Turkey, Blanch checked out of a hotel and jumped in a taxi as a bellboy pushed his luggage out to the curb. At the terminal Blanch started banging on the taxi's trunk as the taxi driver pulled off without handing over the luggage. A quick trunk check showed that the bellboy had forgotten to load the luggage. Blanch missed his flight and returned to the hotel to pick up his belongings.

Road Warrior

Unlike Eudora Welty's stranded traveling salesman, Roger Meryman has the advantages of a cellular phone to bail him out of car trouble. But when debris punctured a tire in a remote Florida area, he discovered cellular service wasn't available. He had to walk three miles to the nearest phone to call AAA.

By the time a replacement tire was found he was already well behind schedule. "I ran into road destruction. Construction workers seem to be tearing up perfectly good roads to block traffic. It takes them too long to reconstruct the road to be worth the effort of fixing a few potholes." Delays included, he drove 13 hours to make a series of appointments. By the time he arrived, everyone had gone home.

On another trip, Meryman was leaving Fort Wayne, Indiana, during a blizzard. He was confident of his ability to navigate a storm but state troopers pulled him over when he tried to enter a closed freeway.

"If you get on this freeway, we'll take you on a ride—straight to jail," they told him when he insisted that he had to catch a plane. He missed the plane.

The Extra Layer

Just about everyone who travels on business likes to tell stories about problems along the way. Of course not everyone wants to have their name attached. A case in point is the San Francisco investment banker who traveled to Chicago to meet with a client. On arrival he was so cold he put on his jogging clothes under his suit and left the hotel for his meeting. When he arrived and the meeting began, he realized there really was no reason for him to be wearing so much clothing. After all, the building was warm inside. But with no time to change, he headed into the meeting and tried to ignore the fact that he was sweating. Worrying that his client would think he was nervous or unprepared actually made him sweat more. An hour into the meeting he passed out, waking to find his client leaning over him, loosening his tie and discovering the layers of clothing beneath his suit. By the time he had taken off a layer, everyone was laughing hysterically.

She Should've Steered Clear

Nancy Anderson used to make her living delivering cars for a driveaway service in New Orleans. "I was feeling under the weather when the company sent me to Cleveland to pick up a car. Airline fares were high at that time. I gave my boss a break and took the bus via a city I always wanted to see, St. Louis."

Anderson's seat was next to a strange young man who babbled constantly with dramatic hand and arm movements, as if preaching to a crowd. His eyes were wild, so as soon as a seat opened up, she moved to the back of the bus, next to the restroom. "I had wanted to see St. Louis for years. Unfortunately at a rest stop during the night, I was tired and sick and did not get off the bus to make my connection to St. Louis." Her new connecting bus was driven by a hastily trained scab taking the place of one of the regular drivers out on strike. Passengers could tell the brakes were dragging but the driver insisted everything was fine. When a car pulled up alongside to explain to the driver that the left rear wheel was on fire, he pulled into a rest stop.

Dressed lightly for the cold weather and shivering, Anderson borrowed a sweater from a fellow passenger. Two hours later a replacement bus arrived and she headed north to Cleveland. On arrival she called her contact again and again. "I finally had to walk a couple of miles through a bad part of town where seedy characters shouted obscenities from passing cars."

She finally found a local bus and took it to a strip mall where she changed buses in the rain. By the time she reached her destination, an office building, the driveaway agency's office was closed. She walked several blocks to a fast-food restaurant. She was out of cash and they refused her credit cards. Back at the office building an employee working late came down, phoned the woman Anderson was supposed to meet and then took her to a burger joint for dinner. "I'll never forget his help."

Back at the office, the agency employee returned with the keys to the car she was to pick up, pointed to where it was supposedly parked and left. Anderson could not find the car. Finally she spotted the vehicle in a satellite lot. The keys worked and the vehicle started. Anderson was on her way back to Louisiana.

Although she was still ill she drove all night. After she delivered the car, a rude cab driver dumped her on the side of the road because she had refused to pay for bad service. She hitch-hiked part way home with a van driver who had a decked out bed in the back. Anderson bailed when he pulled in for gas. She rode the rest of the way home with two young boys transporting a back seat full of guns and an obnoxious dog.

"I only cried once through the entire three day ordeal," says Anderson, who would have been a lot happier if the company she drove for hadn't gone out of business, leaving her empty handed for the entire trip. She wasn't even reimbursed for bus fare.

She Got the Drift

Girl Scout executive Caryl Mallory enjoyed working in western Montana, even in the winter when whiteouts made driving treacherous. She learned how to pull her car out of snow-drifts in deserted areas and make it down the road on Super Bowl Sunday when all the snowplow drivers were on break. Once, after hitting a deer, she thought she was going to have to kill it with a pocket knife to relieve its sufferings. But when she got close, it took off, much to her amazement.

One of Mallory's favorite assignments was camp promotion nights. Prior to one event in Kalispell, she had plenty of time to check on the association's Camp Westana in Olney.

On this particular night there was a foot and a half of snow on the ground. Eager to avoid the slow trek in via the snow covered road, she parked on the highway and went down an embankment, sinking into the deep snow up to her thighs. After toppling over several times, Mallory realized she wasn't well dressed for her trip.

"I got down to the camp, checked everything out and headed back to the car." Back at the car she realized her keys were lost in the snow. After several vain efforts to find her car keys she walked back to the camp office and called a locksmith. She stood outside her car for an hour and an half, waiting for the locksmith to arrive. "Not one person stopped to ask if I was OK." She made it to her promotion night cold and hungry. "Everyone was impatiently waiting for me to arrive, wondering where I was."

Worth the Wait

Jean Richardson who winters in Houston and summers in Trapper Creek, Alaska, frequently, flies back and forth for speaking appearances. Delayed by engine trouble on a flight from Houston to Anchorage via Salt Lake, the plane was towed back to the gate for repairs three times in three hours. Shortly after the passengers were released and told to seek other flights there was an unexpected announcement from the gate agent. The plane was now ready to board. "As we taxied out for the fourth time," says Richardson, "everyone fell silent. You could almost hear people praying. Something must have helped because that plane took off and flew to Salt Lake without a single problem." She missed her connection to Anchorage by five minutes and ended up with a nine-hour delay for her next flight.

Richardson sat down in the terminal and opened her briefcase. "There, right on top, was a picture my illustrator had given me the day before. We had been speaking at an elementary school when she handed me a rough sketch of an old snake with glasses. She said she had seen the snake in a dream the night before, and wanted me to write a story about it." At first Richardson rejected the idea. But as she looked at the picture, an idea came to mind. "During the nine hours I wrote a children's book, all in rhyme, which I called, *When Grandpa Had Fangs*. That book is now in print, and is doing quite well. If not for that miserable nine-hour layover, that book would never have been written."

Cardless from Seattle

For Evelyn Wootton of Port Ludlow, Washington, a thousand miles from home, $2.50 in her wallet, no usable credit cards and no checkbook, her own efficiency had led to trouble.

The artist/freelance journalist was ready for a perfect working vacation— a horseback pack trip with five other artists into the Gros Ventre Wilderness, roughing it for a week at over 9,000 feet near the Continental Divide east of Jackson Hole, Wyoming.

"I had camped in the high country of Wyoming and Colorado years before and I promised myself at least two oil sketches a day of the magnificent scenery. I sacrificed the space for extra clothes and took all the art supplies I could possibly need in a duffel bag that would fit into the panniers on the pack horses.

"My wallet also needed the leanest of packing. In a slim flat case that held only six credit cards I put the card that I use for business expenses, two gasoline credit cards — Chevron and Texaco — my telephone credit card, my roadside emergency card and my driver's license. With $150 in traveler's checks and $50 in cash I was confident that I was prepared to handle anything."

Planning to spend her first night enroute to Jackson Hole in Seattle, she arrived at her motel at a reasonable hour. All seemed well.

"My careful plans began to fall apart when I checked in. My credit card was no good! I soon realized what happened. I didn't destroy the old card when I got the new one, and I had put the expired card in my wallet."

Returning home to get the new card was not the solution. "On the back of my card was an 800-Customer Service number. An agent advised me to send a fax with my signature, all the necessary information, and the address in Wyoming where they could send me a replacement card. Luckily the motel had a fax, but it used another $2 of my dwindling cash reserves. Lodging and dinner that night took a generous bite out of my emergency cash, but with the assurance that my new card would be waiting for me at my motel in Jackson when I returned from the high country, I confidently spent more on dinner and the motel the next night in Missoula.

"I had another drain on my cash reserves. After leaving Spokane I found that in Idaho, Montana and Wyoming there are no Chevron or Texaco stations. Most gas stations accepted Visa or MasterCard, but my card was no good. I skipped the side trips and kept a nervous eye on the gas gauge."

Wootton met her friends and they went on their pack trip as planned. After a glorious week in the high country she arrived back in Jackson on a Saturday night — and no credit card was waiting. She retrieved her wallet and found that her funds totaled $8.50. Another call to the credit card's 800-Customer Service number offered no options except getting her account balance or reporting a lost card.

She discovered that her card had not been sent because cards are not mailed to post office box numbers and all mailing addresses in Jackson are post office boxes.

"After talking to several supervisors of ascending rank I was assured that they could get another card to me, but it would take four days. Meanwhile, I owed for two nights in the Antler Motel in Jackson, and at the height of the tourist season I had no reservations to stay there longer or anywhere else. I also had the bleak prospect of driving 600 miles with no way to buy gas.

"Reason told me that consuming part of my $8.50 for something to eat couldn't make my situation any worse. I went out to eat, relax and consider my options. I could call my daughter in Philadelphia and ask her to wire me money, but it was Saturday night and she could easily be out of town. Both my banks and my stockbroker were closed until Monday. My son was living in Alaska. He could wire me money, but he was in the process of moving his family to Oregon and might not have funds readily available on a weekend. I didn't bring a checkbook, because in the tourist season most places will not accept out-of-state checks."

When Wootton returned to her motel room, there was a message waiting that the credit card company had approved her credit for two nights' lodging. She would be able to check out in the morning, but still had to solve the problem of getting to Spokane. The motel manager came to her rescue with a $20 advance. Thanks to that and a stockpile of cheese, crackers, fruit and soft drinks, Wootton made it home 19 hours after leaving Jackson.

"Before falling into bed I found my good credit card and destroyed the old one."

Blowing in the Wind

When Grand Junction, Colorado, developer Don Bremer decided to mix business and pleasure, he never imagined what could happen on the way to a hotel project in Muncie, Indiana. On the second day of his trip, driving across Kansas with his family, high winds knocked suitcases off the roof of the car. For the next hour, the Bremers were running back and forth across the interstate trying to salvage belongings blowing in the wind. "The kids helped us as best they could but after an hour we were just worn out, running back and forth across the median, dodging cars and trying to grab clothes on the fly. Nothing stayed put." It was quite a scene for passing motorists and truckers as they watched Don and his family scrambling about for shirts and socks, pulling his wife's bra off a fence post and her panties from the cornstalks. "We never did find everything," says Don. "Kansas is a pretty big state."

13

The Globetrotter:
Number One to Madagascar

UNCOMFORTABLY WARM on a delayed shuttle flight from Washington's National Airport to New York, Marcia Wick removed her suit coat and placed it beneath the seat. The aisles were full of unhappy passengers trying to learn why their takeoff was on hold. The little guy to the right was screaming about a bladder problem.

"Mom, I gotta go!"

His mother tried to quiet him, realizing that they could not make it down the crowded aisle to the bathroom. The boy quickly took the matter into his own hands and peed all over Wick's business jacket, her expensive jacket, the only one she had brought along from Seattle for a three week business trip to Madagascar.

Unable to get to the bathroom herself, Wick wasn't sure what to do. "Women worry a lot about minor items such as smells," she recalls, "but I tried not to fret. As soon as I reached JFK I knew I could go to the ladies room and try to wash the urine out." There would be plenty of time for the soaked jacket to dry out on the 52-hour trip ahead to Paris and exciting Madagascar.

Marcia Wick is not a wimp. She spent seven years circum-navigating the globe on her sailboat. She is the author of two yachting guides and her Seattle-based enterprise, Wick Asso-ciates, plans voyages and creates product marketing materi-als for both expeditionary and mainstream cruise ship vessels. She's the person who locates the irresistible destinations that turn stay-at-homes into globetrotters. They'll do anything, even go through credit card meltdown just to follow in her footsteps on journeys of a lifetime. She's visited 124 countries, traveled in war zones after military coups, been shot at on the Mekong River, ridden around Afghanistan in a gasoline-leak-ing truck and snorkled with large sharks.

"But it really pisses me off," she admits, "to have my jacket pissed upon."

In New York she missed her overnight flight to Paris. Her husband, who was supposed to meet her at the gate in New York and come along for the first week of the trip, was a no-show. At the last minute she found another flight to France, but there were no seats available. By now Wick was panick-ing. This was the only plane that could connect with her once-a-week flight from Paris to Madagascar. Finally, for a mere $2,500, she was able to buy the last first class seat on the plane, boarding 15 seconds before the 747 pushed away from the gate.

"Do you smell something odd?" asked the man seated next to her.

"No," she told him. "It's your imagination. Airlines don't recirculate air enough."

The man turned out to be a serious night owl with stereo headphones that blasted heavy metal for most of the flight to France.

In Paris an immigration official looked at her 48-page fold-out passport with neat stamps from around the world and directed her to a special customs line. Traveling isn't easy when you fit the profile of a world class jewelry smuggler. After insisting she was too weak to lift her 100 pounds of luggage onto a table for inspection, the officials hoisted the two suitcases themselves. Neither could believe a woman would travel on her own to Madagascar. And when they asked to see her onward ticket she explained that it was waiting at the Air Madagascar counter.

One of the officers was unable to verify this information on the phone. "There is no Air Madagascar counter," he told her.

Moments later, Wick was released into a scene that looked more like the mosh pit of a rock concert than a late 20th century European air terminal. Early September is the time when many Parisians are inbound from the Côte d'Azur, Americans are outbound back to New York and every other nationality is in transit somewhere. Throngs of relatives awaited arriving flights. The crowds were cheek-to-jowl, dressed in everything from bright yellow-and-red African robes to blue Sikh-turbans and saffron saris, to the skinny khaki shorts of underdressed Scandinavians, the sloppy T-shirts of inebriated British sports fans, and the bright-colored back-packs of young Americans looking dazed and bewildered.

Heading outside to the curb, Wick found a luggage cart and proceeded toward the Air France counter. She felt like she was swimming upstream for an hour toward a waterfall of disinformation. The directions were vague. She knew there was a ticket waiting for her at the Air Madagascar counter, which, as far as she could tell, did not exist. And her feet hurt.

By now Wick had been sitting in aircraft or walking in high-heeled shoes from her last business meeting in Washington, D.C., for 24 hours. Her feet were swollen. As she unzipped her duffel and traded her high-heeled shoes for loafers, a dozen little girls in twirling skirts hemmed with pretty coins rushed toward her bag and helped themselves to gifts for her Madagascar business associates. As she moved through the Charles de Gaulle terminal, a man kept plucking at the black laptop case slung over Wick's shoulder. She turned and gave him an elbow in the shoulder. Quick and evasive, he made a second attempt, then another before heading downstream for easier prey.

Finally, after considerable effort, she found the Air Madagascar counter, which had just opened up. Her husband was there, looking well-rested with a single bag at his side.

"Where have you been?" Then, sniffing the air, he added: "Something smells funny."

"I got laid-up in Washington, D.C."

"'Laid-up'?"

Twelve hours later in the Madagascar capital of Antananarivo, aka Tana, Wick reviewed the advance scouting itinerary prepared for her cruise ship client. Because most of her clients are fussy types searching for something completely different, there's no way Wick can tout Bora Bora (yawn), Australia's Great Barrier Reef (over-rated) or any Western Mediterranean port (way overpolluted). Bali (been there, done that) is often not of interest for the jet set passengers booking with this expeditionary cruise line. These exclusive and expensive ships specialize in little-known destinations such as Petropavlovsk, Funafuti, Vava'u, Chuuk, St. Helena, Broome or Torshavn. Determined to be first in the marketplace by reaching an exotic destination first, companies hire peripatetic Wick to find destinations well off the beaten track. Her three-week trip to Madagascar included 17 domestic flights as well as meetings with 98 people including port agents, research scientists, government and U.S. Embassy officials.

The first thing Wick did after checking into her Hilton Hotel room in Tana was to soak her smelly jacket in the tub. She and her husband fell asleep before having a chance to pull it out to dry. The following morning they forgot about the jacket in their haste to make a dawn rail excursion down to the coast. They were accompanied by Wick's local tour operator and guide, Monique (not her real name).

By the end of the 12-hour train ride, Wick could barely hobble. Shooting pains in her back and lower thighs put a temporary hold on the nonstop Wick itinerary. A doctor arrived at her hotel room and began gently probing the back of her legs, offering a French diagnosis that no one could understand. Slowly, with the help of Monique, who had made an instant transformation from guide to nurse, the doctor pulled down Wick's bed sheets to bare her bottom.

As Wick realized he was moving in with a suppository, she shouted: "No! Americans don't do this!" Then she spun over and pulled up the sheets.

The doctor compromised on a yellow oral medication poured from a quaint set of small glass vials. The acrid mixture promptly knocked Wick out and 12 hours later she was her old self.

With the help of Monique, Wick and her husband flew in and out of Tana, scouting the country for dramatic anchorages, villages that would allow foreigners to shoot locals with their Nikons, prime bird watching spots and Zodiac landing sites. The trip was moving along nicely. Wick was even enjoying the luxury of her fine jacket, which had miraculously appeared several days later at the Hilton room, clean, ironed and odorless. However, Wick learned she would have to speak French (her second language) for the entire three weeks as the tour operator's English was minimal.

By now her husband was beginning to feel pissed off. Even though the two Americans traveled as VIPs whose tour operator could bump locals off flights for their high-priority surveillance missions, he wanted to slow the pace. He failed to appreciate the demands of a fast-paced scouting trip. There were too many meetings, too many nights watching his note-taking wife commune with her laptop. He didn't speak French, which meant he missed out on most of Marcia and Monique's discussions. And this was, after all, his vacation.

"Can't you just cancel all the meetings tomorrow, and we'll go to the beach?" he asked the day before his return to Seattle.

"You know I can't," said Wick. "This is the only chance to scout Nosy Be."

"OK, I'll go to the beach myself."

Wick knew this scouting trip was not healthy for their marriage. Her husband left the next day and she actually breathed a sigh of relief. "Sort it out at home."

As it turned out, he left just in time. Wick's research suddenly took a turn for the worse. Left alone in Nosy Kumba by her local guide, who decided to break for lunch, she headed out into the famous park to photograph the exotic tamish lemurs.

These mammals, which look like a cross between a monkey and a fluffy long-tailed cat, appear cozy enough to curl up next to a child in a crib. As Wick began shooting a black lemur for a brochure and slide show, she began waving bananas to draw a small crowd. Suddenly, lemurs jumped down from the tree tops, landing on her head and back, scratching her arm and knocking her Raybans to the ground. A moment later three hungry lemurs were clawing at her pant legs and ripping open the back of her shirt.

Later, explaining to Monique how she shook the lemurs

by cleverly tossing the bananas to the ground, Wick realized the day was only half done.

"Don't worry," said Monique a little while later at a local beachfront cafe where the owner patched up Wick's clawed wounds. "This afternoon, we have a nice relaxing Zodiac excursion to a nature reserve that you can test for your passengers." For days Monique had been troubleshooting the most delicate problems, making sure that Wick's big and little needs were met. And now, in the company of a Malagasy Zodiac pilot, they were off to visit the famed Lokobe Nature Reserve.

Twenty minutes later, after zipping out across a broad bay, the outboard came to a clunking halt.

"*Pas d'eau,*" explained the pilot. The Zodiac, running behind the ebbing tide, had run aground. Three miles from the coast, the only solution was to quickly push the vessel out into the receding water. But they couldn't budge the outboard driven vessel and it would be five hours before the tide returned to float off the threesome's boat. Squinting in the bright sunlight, Wick looked at the mangrove swamps some 2½ miles away.

The two women began a forced march across the wet sands. Monique was fine in her bare feet. She simply carried her elegant heeled sandals. But Wick's yachting moccasins kept filling with sand and rubbed her feet raw. Two hours later they made it back to dry land.

"Here we are," said Monique with a flourish, "in the Lokobe Nature Reserve. Let's go along this path to see the lemurs."

Minutes later Monique put a finger to her lips and proudly pointed to a pair of lemurs mating in the crook of a tree.

"Look over there," said Monique gesturing toward a dramatic scene that prompted Wick to reach for her camera bag. This was truly a moment in time. A mother lemur was jumping through the trees with a baby clinging to her back. Three juveniles raced across the treetops like Olympic athletes trying to outdo each other with tail-hanging stunts. The two women hunkered together, mesmerized by the arboreal family life of lemurs on full display.

Unfortunately, the banana-bound lemurs Wick had tempted that morning had destroyed both her camera lenses. This time, at least, the beautiful scene would survive only in memory.

By now light was fading. Unlike the waiting Zodiac pilot, who would make it back to port compliments of the flooding tide, the two women would have to walk, barefoot across sacred ground.

Shoeless out of religious respect, without food, water, flashlights or insect repellent, they trekked through the mangrove swamps, tripping on sticky branches and roots. The women held hands to make sure they wouldn't lose each other as they stepped farther into this Tolkien nightmare. By now the mosquitoes had descended. The initial buzz was followed by a Mogadishu style assault. "My feet were slipping and sliding amongst the mangrove roots," says Wick. "It was pitch black. I held a hand out in front of me, sweeping the pathway in front of my face in the manner of a blind person. The only thing bringing me through was Monique."

The women arrived at a campground, where the guide borrowed a car and drove Wick straight to the best hotel in Nosy Be. A few days later both women took a taxi to Montagne d'Ambre Park, rolling in laughter as they discussed every past boyfriend, lover and husband in French. At the park they walked through rain forests, visited a waterfall and scouted for more lemurs. But when the visit ended in the pouring rain, the taxi was nowhere to be found in the deserted park. Monique, her lips turning blue from the cold, dozed against a log as Wick hummed old John Denver tunes imagining that this was what hypothermia meant. Wick was in near panic over her friend's lack of movement. This, she thought, was what hypothermia really meant. But when the driver finally showed, Monique revived herself instantly:

"You want lunch? Picnic?" In a second, the guide who had appeared to be slowly freezing to death popped back up as if nothing was wrong. She instinctively reached into the car and invited the driver to join them for spicy chicken legs, ratatouille, potatoes, sweets and wine. "It was all served," recalls Wick, "on the same moss-covered log where I thought Monique was going to die."

The trip home was slowed when the taxi became mired in the mud. After slipping and sliding and venting dark clouds of exhaust with the two women pushing, the car gained some traction and spewed out a five foot high shower of mud, completely covering both women. Partially blinded, Wick slipped into the muck while Monique continued pushing the car uphill. On the ride home Monique carefully rearranged her hair, which looked like it was covered in chocolate pudding.

During her final days in Madagascar, Wick had a chance to encounter two other famous island species. On a nocturnal chameleon hunt, a local family led the American through a thicket without even using their own flashlights.

"Here he is *madame*," the leader announced proudly, lifting the chameleon off a tree limb and placing the reptile on her arm. Wick shined her flashlight on the animal who looked like a fat, green-coiled snake. A moment later he stretched his scaly body all the way down her forearm. Near her fingers she could see his pointed snout and two front-leg pincer-like claws His long tail relaxed slightly over her elbow. The chameleon clawed at her fingertips and shifted his body over her arm, equivalent to 20-grit sandpaper abrading the flesh of a virgin zucchini.

After the family replaced the reptile on his tree perch, Wick gratefully handed them a large tip. "I would far rather see them show visitors such as me this creature of the dark, than have him eaten at a family banquet, or have the forest destroyed by slash-and-burn techniques so common in Madagascar."

Two hours after this forest episode, Wick's right arm was throbbing and swollen from chameleon scratches. One of the family members applied a poultice resembling boiled chicken feathers and herbs glued together with honey. It eased the discomfort and she slept well.

Waiting to board an airport taxi on her last night in Madagascar, Wick reached for her luggage when she spotted the largest cockroach in the world and respectfully jumped back out of the way.

The taxi driver laughed, swatted the four-inch beast aside with a kick of his shoe and asked:

"Hey, lady, where you go? America, yes?"

He turned to his fellow taxi drivers. "Maybe she like companion?" He rushed around to the front of his vehicle and snatched the roach.

"You like," he asked, waving the cockroach in Wick's face. The roach hissed, its feelers wildly flapping. The other cab drivers laughed. He asked for a moment of silence and told the American woman this was not a joke.

"Madame, you take. Take him to America. He is museum piece. For study. For science."

Then he knelt down by Wick's bags, zipped open an exterior compartment and tucked the roach inside. Before she could protest, a fellow driver had loaded her bags into the trunk. All she could do was close the door and look away as the drivers in the taxi line waved and yelled a friendly: *"Bon Voyage."*

At the stifling airport it was Monique, once again, who parted the Red Sea. With the help of a colleague, she whisked the Seattle-bound bags off to check-in. There was no time to protest about the four-inch hitchhiker. Besides, reasoned the savvy traveler, the less said about the cockroach, the better. Monique hurried her American friend around the long immigration lines. Then she walked the cruise scout onto the plane and gave her the ultimate going away present—a free upgrade to first class. She was still there waving as the plane pulled away.

"Tears were in my eyes," says Wick. "Madagascar? Yeah, well, it was only a business trip."

Postscript from Marcia Wick: "The world's largest cockroach is alive and well and living in Madagascar. A baggage handler there opened the zipper to pilfer my trinkets, and got the surprise of his life. The six cruises turned out to be winners for the company. That is, after the 'bugs' were worked out."

14

The Final Chapter: Stolen Moments

"Life imitated art for Roger Rapoport this weekend, but he'd
just as soon it hadn't. While he was busy selling a book about
bad trips, somebody stole his car."
> —Christian Bohmfalk
> *Denton, Texas, Record-Chronicle*
> December 9, 1997

"I CERTAINLY HOPE this doesn't give you a bad impression of
Denton," said my hostess Donna Morris at the Redbud Inn. I
was traveling light, for a change. Checking in with only the
clothes on my back, I arrived at the Redbud two hours late.
On my previous stop, the sixth of my 11-store book tour of
northern Texas and southern Oklahoma, my rental car had
been stolen from the Hastings parking lot. Two bookstore
employees, wearing *I Should Have Stayed Home* buttons on
their lapels, earlier in the evening had helped me comb the
large lot for the missing Dodge Stratus containing 150 RDR
books, my laptop with the in-progress manuscript and notes
for this book, a Nikon camera and all my clothes. After the
police took my report, one of the employees gave me a ride
over to the B&B. Police Officer Scott Miller told me one to
two cars a week were permanently borrowed from lots in this

shopping center complex. Tonight, no posse was being organized. The long arm of the law appeared to have a very short reach. The odds of ever seeing my belongings were so low that the police didn't even assign an officer to work my case. "We'll just put it on the computer network as a stolen vehicle and wait to hear," Denton Police Lt. David Wright explained.

The following morning my story dominated breakfast conversation at the Redbud's handsome breakfast table. While I finished my tea, volunteers scurried about the inn, putting finishing touches on this landmark, a highlight of the annual Denton Christmas Home Tour. The aroma of freshly baked cookies made the kitchen inviting, and soon there would be hot cider all around. Donna's husband John, a chemist and retired marketing man who traveled extensively, understood. He had already lent me a razor, shaving cream and a toothbrush, suggested where I could begin to replace my missing wardrobe and, best of all, offered to drive me to the Dallas airport to pick up another rental car from National.

At the counter, the National crew handled the problem as smoothly as if it were a flat tire. Within minutes they had taken down the police report number and I was on my way to the jammed Grapevine Mills Shopping Center in a larger Chevy Lumina. There was no charge for the upgrade. (The hardball letters from National's claims department were months away.) An hour later I walked out with the wardrobe I needed to finish the last five stops on my book-signing tour that included Paris, Texas, and the friendly town where Garth Brooks grew up, Yukon, Oklahoma.

Heading up the interstate, I realized all business road warriors live just moments away from disasters we'd rather not think about. And, of course, isn't that the whole point of traveling for a living? The road is our mantra. All we need to do is peacefully continue on our way, tell the truth to all who care to listen and life will be good. If not today, perhaps tomorrow. Om.

Nearly all my stolen property was insured, my manuscript for *After the Death of a Salesman* was backed up on computer disks and missing notes could be reconstructed with a little help. Yes, there were small personal items, undeveloped film of my Uncle Ken's 70th surprise birthday bash in Detroit, a letter to my son and postcard to my daughter, a key ring given to me by my 8-year-old friend William Ferriby, gifts from Hanukkahs past, a letter from a 90-year-old relative about my grandfather's family, small items that would slip far below the adjuster's desk at Hartford Insurance. But anger made no sense. In the weeks ahead, fellow travelers around the country would read wire service accounts of my disaster and send me their own horror stories, a number of them in the book you are now reading. Others will be included in the next volume in this series. Thanks to their inspiring survival stories, I know for sure that there is life after the death of a salesman.

As the sun set over the interstate, I drove north across the Oklahoma border, carefully balancing a takeout container of chicken parmigiana on my lap. I ate slowly to make sure I didn't damage my new wardrobe. My route led through twinkling towns graced with brightly lit parks, nice buildings and even old Model T's for the holidays. My bookstore radar was working, and despite last night's problem, I would be able to make tonight's signing on schedule.

Driving into Duncan, Oklahoma, I wondered if the thieves would give RDR Books away for Christmas or Hanukkah. Were they into children's picture books with a bovine theme such as *Milton* or did their taste run to World War II coming of age memoirs like *Places of Greater Safety*? Entire lives could be found between the covers of this stolen property that might have already been fenced at a used bookstore.

Who, I wondered, got my unabridged audiotape set of Barbara Tuchman's *Distant Mirror* that belonged to the Berkeley Public Library? Perhaps the Middle Ages were too far out of the mainstream to compete with Willie Nelson on the Dodge's tapedeck. Then again, Denton was a college town. Perhaps a history major played Tuchman nonstop on the long ride down to the Mexican border.

Some Denton police officers suspected that the Dodge had been dismantled at a Dallas area chop shop and sold to parts houses piecemeal. The optimistic folks at National were convinced the car would show up in a matter of days. I wasn't sure whom to believe. But I felt better knowing that two nights later the next author signing at the Denton bookstore where my luck had run out wouldn't have to worry about a repeat performance. Security is no problem when your name is Jimmy Carter.

Author's Note

Driving up California's Big Sur Coast on a sales trip in early 1997, I was surprised by the lack of traffic. Because I had left early without reading the morning paper, I didn't realize that a fire in the Ventana Wilderness, supposedly under control, had flared back up. And as I approached the community of Big Sur helicopters ferrying water scooped from the ocean to the fire lines passed overhead. By the time I reached my destination, the Phoenix Gift Shop, it was obvious that the fire crews were back on the job. This was obviously an appointment due to be canceled.

Incredibly, my buyer Karen Trotter was there and when I offered to reschedule she asked for the RDR catalog. The appointment was on. "I'm sorry if I seem a little distracted," she said when I had finished presenting the last of my books. "You see my husband is up there on the fire line driving a bulldozer."

In a way her story was a metaphor for so many of the people who helped make this project happen. Booksellers and reps, marketing executives and buyers, owners and employees, friends old and new, family, editors and colleagues from jobs gone by all turned from their own corporate fire lines at work and home to generously offer their time, their recollections and in some cases their files. Many, of course, are named in these pages but I want to thank them all for making room in their busy schedules for *After the Death of a Salesman*.

Bob Drews, who edited this book, designers Jennifer Braham and Paula Morrison, Erin Perry and Dawn Gray who researched many of the stories and worked with the contributors all deserve special thanks. Martha Ferriby and William Ferriby (who will probably never forget the glow of the Macintosh Powerbook in the campground at Sleeping Bear), Calvin and Florence Goodman, Ken and Yetta Goodman, Margot Lind, Jonathan and Elizabeth Rapoport, Ron and Joan Rapoport, Carla Rapoport and Philip Milner-Barry were particularly helpful. I also want to thank my colleagues at RDR Books, Linda Cohen and Rick Mok. In addition I would like to acknowledge the following people who have helped make this book possible: Susan Adamson, Liz Altieri, Larry Bleiberg, Christian Bohmfalk, Mary Jane Bouchet, Dawn Britt, Lee Broadt, Maureen Colgan, Peter Collier, Denise Dodini, Thelma Elkins, David Garber, Beth Grossman, Richard Harris, Sherlie Lee, Noni Kemball, Bob Koen, Shelia Kowalsky, Mark Livesay, Dick Lombardi, the staff of MAC Computers, Sheridan McCarthy, Susan MacDonald, Bernice Martinez, Karilyn Roberts and the staff of Aero Corporation, David Rickabaugh, Andy Ross, Stan Sesser, Jeff Scott, Lee Stern, Kay Stevens, Jeanne Trinkle, Pam Tulner, Bob Tyrell, Lu Walls and Andrew Wooldridge.

I also want to thank the Denton Police Department, the Redbud Inn, Maura McCann and Jack Fritschi, and Sandra Bray of Hartford Insurance. Still no word on that stolen Dodge Stratus, but thanks for your help.

Also, a word to all the people who generously contributed their stories to this book: I can never thank you enough.

And, of course there's my father, to whom this book is dedicated. He was the first business traveler I ever knew. His pioneer work on technology that helped make the jet age a reality put him on the road a good deal. Many years ago he took me on the first business trip of my life. I got to tag along on a one day flight to New York. Of course it went flawlessly.

HAD A BAD TRIP?

We want to hear all about it. Please mail your travel disaster story to RDR Books at 4456 Piedmont Avenue, Oakland, CA. 94611. If we decide to publish it in the next volume in our series of horrible travel experiences, we'll be in touch. *Bon Voyage!*

I've Been Gone Far Too Long

Scientists' Worst Trips

Edited by MONIQUE
BORGERHOFF-MULDER *and*
WENDY LOGSDON

In this hilarious anthology,
26 research scientists go off
the deep ends of the earth.
Travel with a young
researcher in Dian Fossey's
camp as she is handed a
gun and told to go out and
shoot a gorilla poacher. See
how a scientist reacts
when he discovers a
poisonous bushmaster in
his bidet. From bush pilots
and endangered species to
Land Rover nightmares,
this hair-raising book will
keep you up past dawn.
This book is a tribute to
the courage of an intrepid
band of researchers who
have risked all to bring
home the truth. Authors are
contributing their
royalties to the Wildlife
Conservation Society.

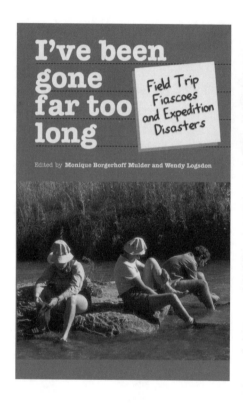

I've been
gone
far too
long

Field Trip
Fiascoes
and Expedition
Disasters

Edited by **Monique Borgerhoff Mulder and Wendy Logsdon**

ISBN: 1-57143-054-7

$15.95
TRADE PAPERBACK
296 PAGES

*"People in khaki and pith
helmets can be funny.
Some could start second
careers as comedians should
they be denied tenure."*
—American Library
Association Booklist

Available at your local bookstore.
For an RDR Books catalog or more information contact RDR Books at:
4456 Piedmont Avenue, Oakland, CA 94611 Ph (510) 595-0595 Fax (510) 595-0598
email: rdrbooks@lanminds.com   website: http://users.lanminds.com/~rdrbooks

I Should Have Stayed Home

The Worst Trips of Great Writers

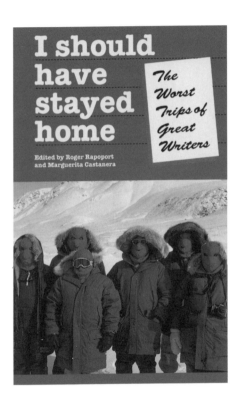

Edited by
ROGER RAPOPORT *and*
MARGUERITA CASTANERA

In this national best seller, 50 top travel writers, novelists and journalists, including **Isabel Allende, Jan Morris, Barbara Kingsolver, Paul Theroux, Mary Morris, Dominique Lapierre, Pico Iyer, Eric Hansen, Rick Steves, Tony Wheeler and Mary Mackey,** tell the stories of their greatest travel disasters. From the electric baths of Tokyo to the *Night of the Army Ants* in Guatemala, this unforgettable book will make you unfasten your seatbelt for the belly laugh of the travel season. Guaranteed to whet your appetite or make you cancel your reservations.

ISBN: 1-57143-014-8

$15.95
TRADE PAPERBACK
256 PAGES

One of "the five best travel books of the year. Feisty, funny, a bracing alternative to the Technicolor-sunset school of travel writing."
—San Francisco Examiner.

Available at your local bookstore.
For an RDR Books catalog or more information contact RDR Books at:
4456 Piedmont Avenue, Oakland, CA 94611 Ph (510) 595-0595 Fax (510) 595-0598
email: rdrbooks@lanminds.com   website: http://users.lanminds.com/~rdrbooks

Others Titles of Interest from RDR Books

Women's Books

A Kind of Grace

Edited by Ron Rapoport

Ron Rapoport, popular commentator on National Public Radio's "Weekend Edition" and Deputy Sports Editor at the *Chicago Sun-Times,* brings together 66 wonderful stories on women athletes ranging from Billie Jean King and Martina Navratilova to the first woman to play high school football. Written by top sportswriters, this remarkable anthology is funny, heartbreaking and beautifully written.

"Good Stuff.... Eloquent.... A powerful argument for gender equity ..."—Jim Murray, *Los Angeles Times*

ISBN 1-57143-013-X
$16.95 Paperback

Places of Greater Safety

By Hilda Hollingsworth

Hailed by critics on both sides of the Atlantic, this coming-of-age memoir tells the hidden story behind the largest evacuation of children ever staged. Hilda Hollingsworth's bittersweet tale shows the courage and ingenuity of young people forced to cope with fear and hardship.

Soon to be a major motion picture.

"Wonderfully written, evocative of its time, funny and sad ...
  written from the courage of the soul."
                        —Dirk Bogarde, *London Telegraph*

ISBN 0-9636161-1-0
$14.95 Paperback

The Virago Woman's Travel Guide to London

By Josie Barnard

London is lustrous, literary and lewd. Josie Barnard captures all the many wonders of this famous city with a special emphasis on women's contributions to London's history, art and culture.

ISBN 1-57143-017-2
$16.95 Paperback

Silvie's Life

By Marianne Rogoff

What do you do when doctors insist your new baby has only a short time to live? Marianne Rogoff answers this painful question in *Silvie's Life,* an autobiography of the heart that appeals to readers of all ages.

"*Silvie's Life* is a tender and beautifully written book. I stayed up all night reading it, absolutely mesmerized, in awe of Silvie's parents and of Silvie herself. I couldn't put it down."
—Anne Lamott

ISBN 1-57143-045-8
$9.95 Trade paperback

Time Pieces

By Rella Lossy

Time Pieces' three sections span four decades of Rella Lossy's life. A prize-winning UC Berkeley poet, Lossy published poetry widely—nationally and internationally. Her experiences with metastatic cancer inspired some powerful and sometimes humorous poems included in the section entitled Metronomes. She succumbed to that disease a week after sending *Time Pieces* to the printer.

"It is very fine poetry, unusual, and should be read."

—Anais Nin

ISBN 1-57143-060-1
$13.95 Trade paperback

Treasure

By Gina Davidson

One of the funniest books ever written about teenagers' parents. Gina Davidson's wry struggle to not be "the world's most hideous mother" of 13-going-on-21 Treasure, and her losing battle to "parent" will bring laughter to readers of all ages.

"A collection of droll essays on raising a teenager in London. Although she wrote some of its pieces for Britain's left-wing *Guardian,* her book is amusing enough to coax a smile out of Newt Gingrich."

—*Cleveland Plain Dealer*

ISBN 1-57143-023-7
$12.95 Paperback

Humor Books

Wannabe Guide to Wine

By Jack Mingo

Do you want impress your friends and humiliate those you don't care for by mastering the art of wine snobbery? In this entertaining book, humorist Jack Mingo can instantly gratify your ambition! Now it's easy to sniff and swirl your way to the top.

ISBN 1-57143-039-3
$9.95 Trade paperback

Wannabe Guide to Golf

By Jack Mingo

It used to take years to sound like a golf pro. Not anymore. Funnyman Jack Mingo will teach you how to achieve your dream in the comfort of your easy chair ... with no green fees to pay! Mingo shows you how to look, act and feel like a putter instead of a putz.

ISBN 1-57143-040-7
$9.95 Trade paperback

Wannabe Guide to Marketing (September 1998)

By Jim Meade

Now you can learn how the pros convince people to buy things they don't really need at prices they can't afford. This book will teach you to sell merchandise you don't even like. Jim Meade finally explains why the marketing department truly rules the world.

ISBN 1-57143-056-3
$9.95 Trade paperback

Books for Children

Time Like a River

By Randy Perrin with Tova and Hannah Perrin

This multicultural first novel written by Randy Perrin with his daughters, Tova, 14, and Hannah, 11, has been hailed by readers across America. This story of two families, one Jewish-American, the other Chinese-American, brought together in a miraculous journey across time and space has captivated readers of all ages.

"A truly amazing accomplishment. . . . The triumph of love over death and the willing of a miracle are important, engaging themes."

—Karen Cushman

American Library Association, Quick Picks Nominee

ISBN 1-57143-061-X
$14.95 Hardcover

The Best of Michael Rosen (Book and Tape)

By Michael Rosen
Illustrated by Quentin Blake
Introduction by Ken and Yetta Goodman

Wetlands Press is proud to offer this exciting poetry anthology by two of the most honored names in contemporary children's literature. Michael Rosen's bestselling titles, such as *We're Going on a Bear Hunt* and *How The Animal Got Their Colors*, have been hailed by critics around the world. Quentin Blake is famous for his award winning illustrations that have accompanied the work of writers such as Roald Dahl.

"Michael Rosen is one of those rare people who have never lost touch with what it is like to be ten. He has the rare ability to convey childhood experience in language as simple and intense as the pleasures and pains it describes."

—*London Times*

ISBN 1-57143-046-6
$16.95 Hardcover

Also available on an unabridged 90 minute audio cassette, read by the author.

ISBN 1-57143-058-X
$11.95

Milton

By Ed Massey
Illustrated by Kristy Chu

Milton, wrapped up in "Cattle Hill," a painting, is off on the ultimate field trip, a story that travels beyond the walls of a museum excursion deep into the American heartland. Evocative of Grant Wood and Virginia Lee Burton, *Milton* is also fine art that celebrates a divine bovine.

Los Angeles sculptor Ed Massey has been praised for his imaginative work that highlights some of the key social and political issues of our day. New York artist Kristy Chu's dynamic paintings and murals have won acclaim from Manhattan to Taiwan. Both hold a Masters in Fine Arts from Columbia University.

ISBN 1-57143-074-4
$19.95 Hardcover

Dinosaur With An Attitude

By Hanna Johansen

Hilarious, mouthy, philosophical—that's compsognathus, the existential dinosaur with an attitude.

"A great deal of dino information is cleverly incorporated into the story."

—School Library Journal

ISBN 1-57143-018-0
$12.95 Hardcover

ISBN 1-57143-022-9
$7.95 Paperback

Dare to Love Us Series

Unloved creatures finally get equal time in this exciting new series. A kinesthetic design lets readers create animal figures by unfolding the pages. Sound chips teach kids how to recognize the distinctive sound of a snake's rattle or a wolf's howl.

The Wolf

By Roger Rapoport
Illustrated by Paul Kratter

Enter the magical realm of one of nature's most fascinating creatures. Learn how wolves help control the balance of nature, sing to one another and use their tails to apologize.

ISBN 1-57143-049-0
$12.95 (Batteries Included)

The Rattler

By Roger Rapoport
Illustrated by Paul Kratter

Here's the book that tells you everything about rattlers: why they shake their tails 50 times per second, eat just once a week, smell with their tongues and listen through their jawbones. Press the button to hear a real snake rattle.

ISBN 1-57143-050-4
$12.95 (Batteries Included)

Available at your local bookstore. For more information or a free catalog contact RDR Books at 4456 Piedmont Avenue, Oakland, CA 94611. Phone (510) 595-0595. Fax (510) 595-0598. Email: RDRBooks@lanminds.com.

See our books on the Web at http: //users.lanminds.com/~rdr-books.